POWER FOR LIVING

Books By T.D. Jakes

40 Days of Power

Help Me, I've Fallen and I Can't Get Up!

Hope for Every Moment

Insights to Help You Survive Peaks and Valleys

It's Time to Reveal What God Longs to Heal

Power for Living

Release Your Anointing

The Harvest

Water in the Wilderness

Woman, Thou Art Loosed!

Why? Because You're Anointed!

POWER FOR LIVING

T.D. JAKES

DESTINY IMAGE® PUBLISHERS, INC.
P.O. Box 310, Shippensburg, PA 17257-0310

"Speaking to the Purposes of God for This Generation and for the Generations to Come."

This book and all other Destiny Image, Revival Press, Mercy Place, Fresh Bread, Destiny Image Fiction, and Treasure House books are available at Christian bookstores and distributors worldwide.

For a U.S. bookstore nearest you, call 1-800-722-6774.
For more information on foreign distributors, call 717-532-3040.
Reach us on the Internet at www.destinyimage.com.

Portions of this text were previously published by Pneuma Life Publishing ISBN 1-56229-434-2; Copyright © 1994 by T.D. Jakes.

Trade paper: ISBN 10: 0-7684-2839-4
ISBN 13: 978-0-7684-2839-1
Hard cover: ISBN 10: 0-7684-2838-6
ISBN 13: 978-0-7684-2838-4

For Worldwide Distribution, Printed in the U.S.A.

Trade Paperback 1 2 3 4 5 6 7 8 9 10 / 15 14 13 12 11 10 09
Hardcover 1 2 3 4 5 6 7 8 9 10 / 15 14 13 12 11 10 09

CONTENTS

FOREWORD .7

INTRODUCTION .9

PART I

CHAPTER 1	Purpose and Power	13
CHAPTER 2	The Power of Why	37
CHAPTER 3	Power to Seek and Find	53
CHAPTER 4	Spirit Power	75
CHAPTER 5	Power and Compassion	89
CHAPTER 6	Victorious Power	113
CHAPTER 7	Power Over Fear	133
CHAPTER 8	Power to Believe	151
CHAPTER 9	Anointed Power	173
CHAPTER 10	Power to Persist and Persevere	195
CHAPTER 11	Go Forth With Power!	215

PART II

POWER PRINCIPLES .235

BONUS MATERIAL

RELEASE YOUR ANOINTING

CHAPTER 1	Power for Living	299

FOREWORD

I cannot think of a greater living example of the consistent ability to draw on the power for living through the anointing of the Lord. T.D. Jakes is a man without equal. There is much we can learn from his words, his spirit, and his passion in delivering the Word of the Lord. Just watching him is a wonder in itself. The presence of the Lord flows freely from him as he teaches. He is simple, clear, and honest in his delivery; sometimes urgent, sometimes gentle, but always accurate and penetrating. He is a man whose inner focus is on the Lord Himself. Even in his most emotional presentation, you can also see the rest and peace in his eyes. The power of the Holy Spirit will always move freely through those who have no other desire than to share the Word of the Lord with hungry people. The *Power for Living* is the anointing He showers His children with. And make no mistake about it; God has much to say to His people. He has much He wants to communicate to the world around us. There is much to learn from the Bishop's words, but also his method, his passion, and his love of the Lord Jesus.

I first met the Bishop at a small conference in the

Pocono Mountains where he was ministering. That was just before he wrote *Woman, Thou Art Loosed!* We literally walked into each other that fateful afternoon in the basement area of the conference center where vendors were displaying their products. The moment I touched him I prophesied about a book churning in his heart. A few weeks later he called me and the rest, as they say, is history.

There are three criteria we use when determining the possibility of publishing a new author. We look at the person, his message, and his ministry. In the Bishop's case, all three were intricately wrapped with integrity, gentleness, and truth. We are proud to offer this work to you. He is a man who has allowed the Lord to mold him into a vessel He can use to change the lives of millions around the world. We are grateful to be part of God's plan for the life of Bishop T.D. Jakes.

DON NORI
Publisher
Destiny Image Publishers

INTRODUCTION

Believers are equipped with the *Power for Living* because of the anointing of the Holy Spirit. Whether or not we make ourselves available to that power is the question.

You are capable of achieving more than you ever imagined by accessing the power that the Lord God has designed especially for you. His Master plan is to carry you to new and exciting heights of splendor, hope, and love.

When economic troubles, family struggles, political upheavals, and natural disasters take center stage, you can rest assured, with an inner peace that passes all understanding, that you have the power to live victoriously through it all. You are the salt of the earth, the beacon in a dark world, the refreshing stream for a thirsty land.

Only through the powerful anointing of the Holy Spirit will the Church forge ahead with power to overcome. As we share our Savior with others, His best flows through us to make the world a safer, stronger, and more beautiful place. A place where children are welcomed, and grandparents are respected; a place where Jesus is Lord and His Kingdom will come.

The power for living is at your fingertips. As you

discover His will for you, keep your heart, mind, and spirit open to receive His anointing. Allow Him to fill you to overflowing, and watch your family, coworkers, and those around you enjoy the glory of God splashing all over them!

40 Days of Power is the companion piece to *Power for Living*. It is filled with thought-provoking wisdom to boost your commitment to living wholeheartedly for Almighty God. The devotional journal is a continuation of the concepts and principles presented in *Power for Living*, and is designed to help you release the power of His anointing in your life. Each day is divided into four inspiring sections: Scripture, Reflection, Power Living Perspective, and Meditation. Each day brings you closer to accepting, internalizing, and releasing the power of His anointing for His glory—and your rich and abundant life.

PART I

CHAPTER 1

PURPOSE AND POWER

And we know that all things work together for good to them that love God, to them who are the called according to His purpose (Romans 8:28).

When we look at the course of our lives, it sometimes appears to be a chaotic path. The course seems to have no certain direction. Yes, even Christians often find themselves questioning the meaning and course of their lives. The things that God does in our lives, and the incidents and situations that happen in many instances, appear to be a haphazard, erratic display of a madman who gets pleasure from seeing his subjects suffer and live in despair.

But with God, this is not the case. There is a reason to the riddle. There is an answer to the question, clarity to the confusion, and calmness in the chaos. A bright new day dawns after the dark night. There is a time and a purpose to everything under the sun, a method to the madness.

Knowing God's divine purpose for your life is one of the greatest assets and enablements to help understand and make sense of the perplexities and complications that seem to overwhelm. People who possess such knowledge possess power. Jesus displayed an assurance of knowing His purpose in life and ministry. When people sought to kill Him for His stand and boldness in declaring the truth, He didn't get fearful and back down from what He had said. No! Jesus stood His ground. Why? He knew His purpose. His purpose was to destroy the works of the devil, not be destroyed by the works of the devil. (See First John 3:8.)

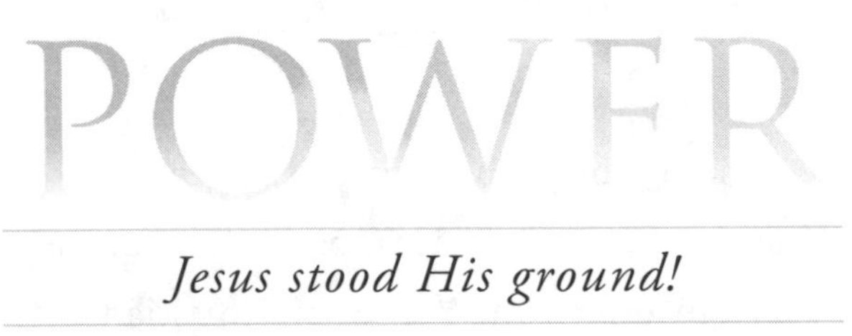

When you are assured of your purpose, you're not fearful of men or external personal conflicts that attempt to hinder you. Why? Because you know with confidence that sooner or later every trial, every hindering situation, and every opposing person and thing in your life will eventually and inevitably bow and submit to God's plan and purpose for your life. It's just a matter of time and circumstance.

The person who knows his or her purpose and God-given vision behaves in a strategic, precise, and decisive manner for spiritual warfare. Paul told Timothy to wage a good warfare by the prophecies that went before him (see 1 Tim. 1:18). When you know your purpose, you won't sit and passively allow things to occur that are contrary to God's purpose and vision for your life. Neither will you be so quick to get discouraged when situations bring conflict and disorder to your life. You know *all* things are working together for your good, because you love the Lord and are called according to His purpose. You don't become frustrated or overwhelmed by those things you can't pray away, rebuke away, cast away, fast away, confess away, or speak away. Why? Because you know that if it's in your life, God has allowed it and He wants to use it (since it's there) to transform you into the express image of Christ. He will bring you into that purpose for which you were created. *All* things, not some, work together for the good of those who love the Lord.

All things work together for good for those who love the Lord.

LIVING

Therefore, if you are confused, ready to give up, wondering what's going on and what all the turmoil and chaos you're experiencing is about, ask God, "Why?" He just might say, "It's about purpose." Maybe He's building a foundation of character in your life. Perhaps it will enable you to obtain the success and blessing that is to be poured into your life. Maybe it is a prelude to the powerful anointing that is about to come upon you.

He's got to teach you how to trust Him now, while you are in the desert, so that when you get into the Promised Land and people start acting funny toward you because they're jealous of the anointing on your life, you won't be afraid to cut the ungodly tie. You know your help comes not from others, but from the Lord. Do you understand what I'm saying? I know you do. If you don't, you'd better ask somebody! But don't just ask anybody, ask the Lord! Call on the Lord and He will answer you. Go ahead. Don't be afraid. Ask Him, "Lord, why?"

POWER

There is a purpose and reason for your life!

LIVING

Why is there so much strain, why so much struggle, so much conflict, why so much hell? Could it be because I am a man or woman of destiny? Could it be because there's a purpose, a reason for my life? Am I going through so much because I was not brought into this earth haphazardly, but because there is actually some divine, ordained logic to my being? Is it true that I'm not some mistake my mother and father made one night in the heat of passion or uncontrollable lust? (If you were born out of wedlock or even as a result of rape, you're not an illegitimate child. What your parents did was illegitimate—you are not. You need to know that as truth.)

You may wonder: *God, is it possible that You have a divine motive, a divine reason for my conception? Am I destined, purposed, called to do something great in life? Is it something that nobody else has done, something that nobody else can do but me? My brother can't do it, my sister can't do it, my husband can't do it, my wife can't do it, my pastor can't do it. Is it something so unique to my personality, so connected to my life experiences, so relative to my sphere of influence, so dependent upon my color and culture, so necessary to my needs and failures and shortcomings that nobody—no one—can do it exactly the way You want it done but me?* God's response: "Yes! You're absolutely right!"

Know that *"to whom much is given, much will be required"* (see Luke 12:48 NKJV). So get ready for the fire!

Declaring the End From the Beginning

Remember this—fix it in your mind and take it to heart:

> *Remember the former things, those of long ago; I am God and there is no other; I am God and there is none like me. I make known the end from the beginning, from ancient*

> *times, what is still to come. I say: My purpose will stand, and I will do all that I please* (Isaiah 46:9-10 NIV).

Wait a minute, God said He is declaring the end from the beginning. That's backward. That's out of sequence. That's out of order. You never declare the end from the beginning. Anybody who tells a good joke will tell you not to tell the punch line before the introduction. But God says, "I'll do it backward for you. I declare the end from the beginning. I don't start at the foundation. I reverse the order. I start with the end of it, then I go back and start working on the beginning and make the beginning work into the end." God says, "I establish purpose and then I build procedure."

God knows you are going to make it!

God says, "I put the victory in the heavenlies, then I start from the earth and move upward. I make sure everything is set according to My design, then I work it out according to My purpose and My plan, My will and My way." That's why God is not nervous when you are nervous, because He has set your end from the beginning. While you're struggling, groping and growling, trying to get it together, and wondering whether you will make it, God knows you're going to make it, because He has already set your end!

A friend of mine once told me how movies are made. I thought the directors shot the movie scenes in numerical sequence, beginning with the first scene and ending with the last. That is not how it is done. Most times they will shoot the final scene of the movie first. They shoot the last scene first, then roll back the film and start shooting from the beginning, making the beginning work its way into the ending.

BUILT FOR A HABITATION FOR GOD

> *Now therefore ye are no more strangers and foreigners, but fellow citizens with the saints, and of the household of God; and are built upon the foundation of the apostles and prophets, Jesus Christ Himself being the chief corner stone; in whom all the building fitly framed together groweth unto an holy temple in the Lord: in whom ye also are builded together for an habitation of God through the Spirit* (Ephesians 2:19-22).

God's approach to destiny is first establishing the purpose, then reverting to the beginning to develop you and instruct you on how to fulfill the purpose. God works out purpose the way you would design and construct a house. If you want to build a massive house, you must first hire an architect. The architect takes the vision you have for the house and transfers it onto paper (a blueprint), establishing what it shall be before it is ever built. Then the carpenter comes in and makes the vision a reality by constructing in material form (manifesting in the present) the design (vision) that the architect has established on paper (the blueprint).

POWER

Anything that is worth having is worth fighting for and worth working hard for.

LIVING

Whenever the builder is confused, he refers back to the blueprint. By looking at the blueprint, he knows whether to order steel beams or wood beams, carpet or tile, brick or stucco. Whenever the builder is unclear about any detail or specification, all he needs to do is check the blueprint and look back at what the architect has declared in the design.

I want you to know that God is the Master Architect (designer) and Master Builder all in one. He never gets confused about what is planned or how it is to be built. When God builds something, He builds it for maximum efficiency and optimal performance. We get confused and doubt the outcome. Discouraged, we often find ourselves asking God, "Why did You make me wait while other people go forth? Why does it take so long for my breakthrough to come?" God responds, "What does the blueprint say? What do the specifications call for?"

Many times we wonder why we go through so much persecution. Why do we experience so much rejection that we often feel alienated by those around us just because we love God and want to do His will? God says, "I'm building a solid foundation so you'll better understand pressure and be able to go through the storms of life without being moved or shaken." God's response is simple. Anything that is made well is made slowly. "Quality must go in before the name goes on." Anything that is worth having is worth fighting for and worth working hard for.

We also have to know that God is not just building any kind of house. God is building a house of glory, a house filled with His Spirit, governed by His Word (will), and submitted to the Lordship of His Son, Jesus Christ. As tenants of that house, we are called to represent the Builder and Lord of that house by manifesting His glory on the earth. God says, "When I get through with you, when I get through nailing on you, when I get through hooking your two-by-fours together and putting windows in, when I get through hanging siding on you and placing bricks on your frame, then you are going to be a glorious edifice, a sight for the world to see." Still the house is not for us to be glorified, but that God might be exalted and glorified. *"We have this treasure in earthen vessels, that the excellency of the power may be of God, and not of us"* (2 Cor. 4:7).

Vision (Revelation) and Purpose

> *Where there is no revelation* [vision], *the people cast off restraint* [perish]*; but blessed is he who keeps the law* [the Word of God] (Proverbs 29:18 NIV).

Solomon declared in the Book of Proverbs that where there is no vision (no divine and fresh revelation from God), the people perish (they lose control and cast off restraint).

If you are a person without direction, purpose, meaning, or understanding of God's specific intent for your life, it could very well mean that you lack vision. You may lack a personal revelation, which is God's divine insight into the reason for your being and the reason for your living. Vision not only gives meaning and understanding of one's purpose in life, it also gives you wisdom about how to bring it to pass. Vision gives understanding and reveals meaning to the trials you may experience at any given time.

POWER

Be a person of vision.

LIVING

God imparts to you a revelation of His plans for your life. That is how vision begins. Then in some cases, God confirms that word He spoke personally to you through a prophecy given to you by another man or woman of God. If you try to figure out the fulfillment of the prophecy by looking at your present situation, circumstance, or condition, it may be hard to believe without the assurance of faith and the witness of the Holy Spirit. Why would it be so hard to believe? Because when God gives you a vision, it is always too great and complex for you in your own power and ability to bring about. *"Not by might, nor by power, but by My Spirit, saith the Lord of hosts"* (Zech. 4:6).

God calls those things that are not as though they were. He calls you, in the present, what you're going to be in the future, and then makes you prove His Word to be true. Hence the Scripture says, *"...Let God be true, but every man a liar..."* (Rom. 3:4). It means you embrace what God has said about you over what everybody else has said about you, good or bad. When all has been said and done, God proves what He has said about you. It comes through His written Word and His personal revelation to you. His Word is right and everyone who speaks contrary to that Word is a liar. Your life will witness the validity of God's Word if you continue to walk by faith and obey the Father. You will prove to this world that God is real and that He is able. There is nothing else in life that pleases God the Father more.

Jesus proved the validity of God's Word when He rose from the dead. This was true regardless of the Romans, Jews, skeptics, and doomsayers who did not believe in His divinity.

My brothers and sisters, you must continue to obey and serve God. You are going to show your critics and the unbelievers that you, as the servant of God, will win in the end. Some critics will bet against you and they will speak against you. They will say, "That girl ain't never gonna be nothing. Her mama was nothing. Her aunt was nothing. I knew her grandmother and she was nothing. Her granddaddy was nothing. Her father was nothing and she is going to be nothing." According to the Word of God, *"If any man be in Christ, he is a new creature: old things are passed away; behold all things are become new"* (2 Cor. 5:17). God said that we are going to make liars out of all of them. He says, "I will remain true, and every man a liar" (see Rom. 3:4).

Some of you have been lying to yourselves, telling yourselves that you're nothing. You are telling yourself you're no good; but you ought to believe God. Believe Him in spite of your feelings or emotions. Stop believing those lying prophecies of the past—relatives and friends who claimed you would never amount to anything. Stop believing people and teachers who called you stupid. Turn a deaf ear to racism that said because you're black you are not important; sexists who said because you're a woman you're not important. Stop believing the lies. Become renewed to the truth of God. You might have had a bad childhood and have been abused, misused, rejected, and neglected. God says forget those things that are behind you and reach forth to those things that are before you. Press toward the mark of your high calling in Christ Jesus (see Phil. 3:13-14).

> *...He is our father in the sight of God, in whom he believed—the God who gives life to the dead and calls things that are not as though they were* (Romans 4:17 NIV).

> *No longer will you be called Abram; your name will be Abraham, for I have made you a father of many nations* (Genesis 17:5 NIV).

"Calling those things that are not as though they were." The emphasis in this particular context is not on Abraham or any believer calling things that are not as though they were, but on *God* calling those things that are not as though they were. It is God, through His Word, speaking into existence

His will, not man's will. We should be very glad that it is God and not man. I wouldn't want a man to have the power to determine my future and destiny.

It is God who calls those things that are not as though they were. Our responsibility is to line up our will with His will. When we do, our lives become empowered by the grace and Spirit of God to accomplish what normally would be humanly impossible. That is the essence of authentic prophecy that comes from the heart of God.

POWER

Stop believing lies!

LIVING

If we continue to walk by faith, believing in the prophetic word that God has spoken over our lives, things that may seem impossible to realize in the natural shall come to pass.

The just shall live by faith, and anything that is not of faith is sin. For we walk by faith and not by sight (the physical senses—emotions, mental reasoning, or the things that we can visibly see). (See Romans 1:17; 14:23; Second Corinthians 5:7.) When God speaks a word into our lives, as far as He is concerned, it has already been accomplished. If the purpose has already been completed, the task or assignment has already been done; it is in essence a finished work. He calls those "things that are not as though they were."

Hebrews 10:14 declares that God offered Christ as the ultimate sacrifice for man's sin and has *"...perfected forever them that are sanctified."* The word *perfected* in this particular passage of Scripture means in the Greek, "to bring to an end by completing or perfecting the accomplishment of bringing to completeness." This simply means that the end is already finished. It came by the supernatural power and grace given to us by what Christ accomplished during His crucifixion and resurrection.

Therefore we no longer have to strive in the flesh in order to fulfill God's purpose. The calling for our lives has already been determined in Heaven. It is a complete and finished work. Your purpose in the sight of God is already an accomplished thing, waiting for your fulfillment. *Perfected* means completely over, settled, done, and concluded. God says, "I have perfected your life and purpose. I have fixed them; I have set their course in stone. You don't have to run and see what the end is going to be." God said that it's already accomplished. The thing you're worried about performing, God said it is already done through His purpose and power.

What about all the debris in your life? What about all of those loose ends and uncertain things that Shakespeare talked about in *Macbeth?* He said, "Life is a tale told by an idiot," but God tells a different story. God says, "All of those foolish things are going to work together for the good of them who love the Lord, to them who are the called according to His purpose" (see Rom. 8:28). To walk with God, you've got to be willing to hear some things that sound foolish. Oftentimes, obeying God does seem like "a tale told by an idiot."

POWER

The thing you're worried about is already done through God's purpose and power.

LIVING

God called Moses from upon Mount Sinai and said, "Come on up here. I'm going to show you My purpose, what My plan shall be."

Moses walked upon the mountain saying, "Yes Lord, what's going on?"

The Lord said, "This is what is about to take place. There's a man down there in your church (camp) named Aaron. Aaron is to be appointed as a high priest. I'm making him an outfit: a garment symbolizing my pattern of holiness, righteousness, and My set and divine way of communicating to My people. The outfit will have a breastplate with 12 stones, each one representing one of the 12 tribes of Israel—My chosen people. I'm getting him together, girding his loins with truth. When I get through with him, he shall be a glorious and beautiful sight for eyes to see. Aaron shall be the one who will be able to go in and out before Me." Anybody could have attempted to go in before God, but it took a holy person to come out still alive. God told Moses that when nobody else could be in His presence and live, Aaron would be anointed to come in and go out alive.

Aaron sounds like a pretty good fellow, but while God was declaring to Moses about Aaron's perfected state, He was already taking care of Aaron's end, calling those things that are not as though they were. Aaron was down at the bottom of the mountain, working on the beginning. If you were to judge from Aaron's beginning, you would not believe what was promised to this guy. As a matter of fact, the guy was down the mountain engrossed in idol worship, worshiping a golden calf. The guy just didn't have it going on. He was an idolater. He was the head of the hypocrites, president of the failures, chairman of the defeated, busy building a golden calf unto a strange god.

When Moses came down the mountain, he began to build up Aaron, exhorting him on who he was and what God called him to do and be. Moses got the revelation of the end. Moses says, "Hey man, (I'm paraphrasing), oohhh God has designed an outfit for you.... Blood, you're going to be laid out, you are going to be too sharp."

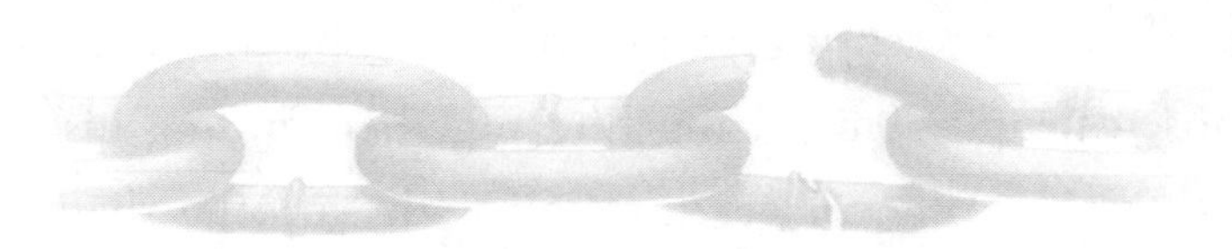

It is wonderful to have a plan, but that means nothing if you have no power to perform the plan and accomplish the purpose. God sends people in and out of your life to exercise your faith and develop your character. When they are gone, they leave you with the enriched reality that your God is with you to deliver you wherever you go! Moses died and left Joshua in charge, but God told him, "*...as I was with Moses, so I will be with thee...*" (Josh. 1:5). Joshua never would have learned that while Moses was there. You learn this kind of thing when "Moses" is gone. Power is developed in the absence of human assistance. Then we can test the limits of our resourcefulness and the magnitude of the favor of God.

I know what you probably would have said about Aaron. Something like, "Lord God, do You know where he is? Do You know what he's doing?" You don't believe God knew what he was doing? Remember, God sets the end from the beginning, calling those things that are not as though they were. God declares even to you today, as you read this book that, "In spite of what you've done, in spite of how you've failed, in spite of how you've messed up, in spite of how you have suffered, in spite of how many times you have given up and almost died, I want you to know that My grace is sufficient for you. My grace will enable you to be victorious and make it through to complete your journey (purpose). I've shed blood for you and given sacrifices for you. When I get through washing, molding, and making you into what I've already declared you are, you will show the world how glorious I am."

POWER POINTS FOR LIVING

1. All things work together for the good of those who love God. Think of three times when God worked something good from something bad.

2. While you're struggling, groping and growling, trying to get it together, and wondering whether you will make it, God knows you're going to make it, because He has already set your end! List several ways you can keep from worrying about a situation.

3. Anything that is worth having is worth fighting for and worth working hard for. Write about something that you want that will take a lot of hard work to get. Are you willing to put forth the effort?

4. Embrace what God says about you over what everybody else says about you,

good or bad. List five things that make you special.

5. Stop believing the lies. Determine to believe the best about yourself. Write about why you will stop believing the lies people say about you—or that you say about yourself.

6. God's grace is sufficient for you. Has there been a tough time—or two—when you realized that God's grace is the only thing that got you through? Write about it.

7. Give God the glory. Thank God for ten things He has done for you today.

CHAPTER 2

THE POWER OF WHY

How long, O Lord, must I call for help, but you do not listen? Or cry out to you, "Violence!" but you do not save? Why do you make me look at injustice? Why do you tolerate wrong? Destruction and violence are before me; there is strife, and conflict abounds. Therefore the law is paralyzed, and justice never prevails. The wicked hem in the righteous, so that justice is perverted.... Your eyes are too pure to look on evil; you cannot tolerate wrong. Why then do you tolerate the treacherous? Why are you silent while the wicked swallow up those more righteous than themselves? (Habakkuk 1:2-4,13 NIV)

WAITING ON GOD FOR AN ANSWER?

Have you been asking God questions about your life and the society in which we live? Why so much heartache, so much pain? Have you, like the prophet Habakkuk, become perplexed, distraught, saddened, grieved, and even angered at the injustices of our day? What about the plight of the poor, the pain of the oppressed, the continual wickedness of humankind, and the hypocrisy and complacency of the Church? Have you cried in the midnight hour and asked God, "How long?" Have you thought, like Habakkuk, that maybe God just was not listening?

Are there problems in your life left unresolved, questions unanswered? Have you considered entering into the courtroom of the Kingdom of God to ask, "God, Your Honor, why? What's going on? What is the purpose? What's happening in my life?"

"Lord, I don't mean to intrude on Your busy schedule, but if You would, please just reveal to me the method to this madness. Your master plan must be a divine strategy."

God says, "Wait on Me, I'm going to answer you. I'm going to speak to you. I'm going to talk to you. I'm going to show you My glory and My power."

POWER

Asking why is not necessarily a rebellious attempt to question God's authority.

Asking *why* is not necessarily a rebellious attempt to question God's authority. Asking *why* is just wanting to understand and be at one with God's reasoning. *Why* is about the children of Israel knowing the acts of God, but Moses knowing the ways (the heart and reasoning) of God. *Why* is a desire for a divine impartation and revelation from God, wanting His mind to be in you, which is the mind of Christ.

Why is saying, "God, I want to be a clone of Your wisdom. I want to draw from Your spiritual and intellectual resources until Your thoughts become my thoughts, and Your ways become my ways, and Your ideas become my ideas. I want a supernatural exchange.

"God, I'm not questioning Your right or ability to rule or govern, but show me the strategy. Show me Your plan and purpose for my life. Let me see the blueprint before the building is built. Let me see the plan before the product is manufactured. I just want to know what I shall be when I get through crying, suffering, and laboring in turmoil and confusion. Every now and then, tell me and remind me how it's going to end!"

You don't feel a great amount of emotional intensity when you read the word *why* or speak the word *why*. But when a sincere, heartfelt, passion-filled *why* comes out of one's heart, it is often the consequence of a certain amount of bewilderment and perplexity. It comes from one who has become distraught, despondent, and discouraged. One that says, "I've reached the end of my rope. I've come to the end of my reasoning and can't understand why. Why must I suffer? Why must I cry? Why must I keep reaching out to people who hurt me? Why am I misunderstood? Why do I keep going through the same things again and again and again? Why do I keep going through periods of prolonged confusion? I'm not saying I'm going to quit or I'm going to backslide. I'm not getting ready to go out, get drunk, throw in the towel, surrender to the temptation and the pressure of satan or the lust of the world. But God, I'm on my knees and I just want to know *why*?"

POWER

I just want to know why.

LIVING

"Why do the wicked seem to prosper over the righteous? Why do the hypocrites seem to get all the blessings, and the real saints go without? Why are the anointed persecuted? Why does there seem to be no justice? Why does the vision tarry? This is an emergency! It's an SOS. It's a 911 call. Lord, I need a breakthrough right now—not tomorrow, not next week, next month, or next year. Lord, I need it now!

"Why is the blessing delayed? Why must I wait? Why do the heathens rage? Great God! Why is there so much hoopla going on in my life? Why do the people imagine vain things? They just make up things, or come up with strange things. Am I in the right place at the wrong time, or the wrong place at the right time? Lord, what's up? Why are the minds of men coming up with all of these illusions to perplex me and disturb me? Why is everybody tripping on me? Why do vain things, empty things, lifeless things, and dead things keep bombarding my thinking and my life? Why, why, why, why, why, why?

"Why have the kings of the earth (men and women of position, prestige, and authority) set themselves against me?

"Could it just be because I am anointed?"

You do know that anointed folks go through more than everybody else, right? I used to have the wrong notion that when you are really anointed, you no longer have problems or rough times. But you show me anybody who's really Holy Ghost, knee-jerking, tongue-talking, casting-out-demons, laying-hands-on-the-sick, miracle-working, world-changing, mind-transforming, mind-boggling, head-straightening anointed, and I'll show you somebody who cried in the middle of the night and suffered all night long, wondering, *Where are You, God? I looked on the right and You were not there. I looked on the left and You were not there either."*

Anybody who's really anointed has suffered some things, has gone without, has been lonely, has agonized, has had to press through, and has crawled a mile or two. But, my friends, I have to confess that through it all I, like the anointed ones, have learned to trust in Jesus. Through it all, I've learned to trust in God. Though He slay me, yet will I praise Him. Why? It's the anointing!

Perhaps you've been bewildered, confused, or discouraged while waiting on God. Have you wondered why your vision tarries or when things are going to start looking up? Why is it taking so long for morning to come? Why is my change not coming forth? If you've been totally preoccupied, consumed, overwhelmed, and overcome with *why* and still have no answers, my beloved brothers and sisters, I can only tell you what God told me some time ago: "Get Ready! Get Ready! Get Ready! Get Ready! Get Ready! Get Ready!"

YOU ARE ANOINTED

> *Why do the heathen rage, and the people imagine a vain thing? The kings of the earth set themselves, and the rulers take counsel together, against the Lord, and against His anointed...* (Psalms 2:1-2).

Why? The word *why* is the request of a student, not merely for an answer, but for the understanding of the procedure that leads to an answer. It is not just a request saying, "Give me the bottom line answer." The student is asking, "Explain the dynamics of the issue, the situation, or the problem until I fully understand in absolute and complete detail the process that leads me to the solution."

Why defined: For what purpose, reason, or cause; with what intention, justification or motive; the cause or intention underlying a given action or situation; a difficult problem or question. *Why* is used to express mild indignation, surprise or impatience.

Why? Every mother will tell you that children go through

a time of asking why. No matter how many answers you give them, they keep asking, "Why?"

"Why is it light outside, Daddy?"

"Because the sun is shining, son."

"Why is the sun shining?"

"Because God wanted the sun to shine."

"Why did God want the sun to shine?"

"Because we need sunlight."

"Why do we need sunlight? Why?"

"Because sunlight helps us to grow."

"Why does it help us grow?"

After this line of questioning, you become exasperated, exhausted, and frustrated. You finally say, "Why do you keep saying, 'Why?' Why do you keep asking me the same thing over and over again? I've given you an answer, but you just keep asking me 'Why?'"

Why does not merely say "Give me an answer." It's a demand, an inquiry, a request that you talk with me, that you dialogue with me until I understand your thought process. It says, "Communicate with me until I understand your wisdom, until I know how to deduce for myself and determine in my mind the things that you have deciphered in your maturity. I know that I may appear to be inferior and my intellect may be less developed than yours, but explain the situation and break it down to my level of understanding that I might be able to determine the matter for myself. That way, when you're not around, I can equate and come to a solution or conclusion on my own without the help of others. I need to think in a decisive manner for myself that I may learn to be independent."

Why? My father said something to me before he passed away. He was on his deathbed and his words changed my life. He was fading away in front of me, as a young man in his early 40s. While I sat at his bedside, my father's words were very simple, yet profound. He said, "Son, I want you to know something. By the time I figured out what life was really all about, it was time to go." That bothered me. That troubled me. That angered me. It really disturbed me.

POWER

"By the time I figured out what life was really all about, it was time to go."

LIVING

I thought, *I don't want to spend all of my life trying to figure out what life's really all about, and by the time I finally realize what's actually going on, it's time to go.* From that moment, I started playing beat-the-clock. "God, I want to know why. I want to know *now*, not when I'm an old man or on my deathbed. I want to be able to decipher, to determine and to realize purpose, to understand what is the true meaning for my existence. Away with the trivialities, the small stuff, the surface stuff, and the superficial issues. I want to know the real deal, the intrinsic nature of the thing. Give me the divine philosophy, the heavenly strategy, and the majestic plan. I want to know what it's really all about. Please God, answer the *why* of the matter."

As mentioned previously, Shakespeare wrote, "Life is a tale told by an idiot." Life, according to Shakespeare, is just a bombardment of separated incidents that have no harmony, relativity, or relationship with one another. It's just this, that, and the other. In life there is no formation, no conclusion, no answer—just a wild man telling a strange story that has no ending, solution, or equation. Life is sporadic, out of control, wild, crazy, and all mixed up. Don't try to figure it out. Just leave it where it is. Don't worry about it. Just lay it down to the side. Don't try to understand anything about what life is really all about.

But Shakespeare's tale was wrong. The question that needs to be answered is, "Why are all the fatalists and misguided doomsayers of the world wrong?" It is this question of the anointed person's unanswered dilemma of joy and pain, suffering and comfort, tragedy and triumph, and that same anointing that gives the believer power for living that this book seeks to address.

Having a Divine Perspective

The writer was wrong in his assessment of life. He sought

to draw a conclusion without acknowledging and inquiring from the One who has given life to all. God is the Creator of all living things. The biblical perspective of life is not one of unfulfilled dreams or unanswered prayers. The biblical, godly perspective of life is one of insight, direction, hope, fulfilled dreams, and visions. Just because the vision tarries doesn't mean God has changed His mind or given up on you. It could very well mean that the timing or the situation is not right for God to get the ultimate glory and benefit out of your trusting in Him. Hold on to faith even in the midst of the battle.

The vision could be delayed because God knows you're not mature enough to handle the success. Perhaps it will result in a new and fresh anointing you've been seeking. Maybe the vision tarries because, even though you're saved, baptized with the Holy Ghost, and a little bit sanctified, your heavenly Father knows there's a part of that old sinful person that hasn't quite died. But, I'll tell you as a living witness, if you hold on and wait a little while longer, your change is going to come. God will come through in the end.

Stand like Shadrach, Meshach, and Abednego. Do not bow to the temptation of others' agendas or to ungodly persuasion. Do not try to keep up with the Joneses or bow to selfish ambition and self-promotion. Do not bow to the spirit of anxiousness and impatience. Continue to walk by faith and not by sight, knowing God is able to do more abundantly and exceedingly than all you could ask or think (see

Eph. 3:20). God is able to finish that good work He began in you when you first gave your life to Him. If you do these things and maintain the faith, regardless of the external circumstances, in time you will come out as pure gold, a vessel of honor.

POWER

The vision could be delayed because God knows you're not mature enough to handle the success.

LIVING

Before we begin our journey into the realm of truth and Spirit, please allow me to say that I do not propose that this one book will answer all the "whys" that preoccupy your thoughts and mind. What I endeavor to do is present you with some basic biblical principles, some precious spiritual jewels that, if acted on, will give you better insight into the heart of your heavenly Father. He desires for us to ask for direction for our lives.

Remember, those who love God with all that is in them and who hold fast to their trust in the Father, can enjoy the saying: Good things truly do come to those who wait. The determining factor is whom you're waiting on. God says

"There is a purpose and a time for all things" (see Eccles. 3:1). There is reason for man's existence. There is some good working out of the matter. There is some logic to the development and a major strategy that causes all of these broken pieces to fit together. If we relate to God like a student to a teacher and ask *why* long enough, and are persistent enough, we will begin to understand what the *why* is all about.

POWER POINTS FOR LIVING

1. Asking *why* is just wanting to understand and be at one with God's reasoning. Have you recently asked God why? What was His answer?

2. Through it all, I've learned to trust in God. How has His answer given you power to forge ahead?

3. Give me the divine philosophy, the heavenly strategy, and the majestic plan. I want to know what it's really all about. Do you understand more about yourself today than last month? Last year? What discoveries have you made?

4. Do not bow to the temptation of others' agendas or to ungodly persuasion. What are you most afraid will happen if you don't do what others' want you to do?

5. Do not try to keep up with the Joneses or bow to selfish ambition and self-promotion. What is the difference between ambition and selfish ambition?

6. Do not bow to the spirit of anxiousness and impatience. List several ways you can overcome these feelings and attitudes.

7. Continue to walk by faith and not by sight, knowing God is able to do more abundantly and exceedingly than all you could ask or think. What are you believing God for today?

CHAPTER 3

POWER TO SEEK AND FIND

I was taught not to ask God, "Why?" I was taught that true Christians never ask God that question. It was considered a breach of our faith to ask it. If you really believe God, you just completely accept everything that comes your way without asking God anything pertaining to its reason for happening—as if God gets insulted, mad, or feels like you're questioning His authority when you ask Him *why*. Others feel that if you ask *why*, God is intimidated with your quest for knowledge or that you might ask Him something that He cannot answer or that you might offend or hinder God's ability to be omniscient. For whatever reason, many feel that they should not ask why of Almighty God.

However, the Bible says, *"If any of you lack wisdom, let him ask of God, that giveth to all men liberally, and upbraideth not..."* (James 1:5). God said, "Come to Me and ask Me why." He said, "I'm not afraid of your questions. I'm not afraid of you." God is not insecure in His sovereignty. He's not envious of us or afraid that His position, power, or authority is going to be jeopardized by you or anybody else knowing too much. I don't care how many times you have to ask Him. He says ask of Him who gives freely as He wills.

God said, "When you are confused, your mind is

perplexed, your heart is troubled, and you don't know what in the world to do, come to Me and ask Me. Lay all the cards down on the table. Say, 'This is happening and that is happening. There's trouble here and there's trouble there. There's trouble everywhere. I've been serving You all I know how, and it looks like things are getting worse instead of better. God, why?'"

POWER

God is not insecure in His sovereignty.

LIVING

God says He can handle it. Bring it to Him. "I'm able," says God, "to share with you the kind of truth that transforms." God says, "Cry out to Me; inquire of Me. Knock and the door shall be opened, seek and ye shall find" (see Matt. 7:7).

Faith in God—The Key to Answered Prayers

God says when you've searched for Him with your whole heart (your entire being), then you will find Him (see Jer.

29:13). If we are serious about hearing from God, we're going to have to exercise the kind of faith that is strong and persistent just like the woman in Jesus' parable about the unjust judge.

> *And He spake a parable unto them to this end, that men ought always to pray, and not to faint; saying, There was in a city a judge, which feared not God, neither regarded man: and there was a widow in that city; and she came unto him, saying, Avenge me of mine adversary. And he would not for a while: but afterward he said within himself, Though I fear not God, nor regard man; yet because this widow troubleth me, I will avenge her, lest by her continual coming she weary me. And the Lord said, Hear what the unjust judge saith. And shall not God avenge His own elect, which cry day and night unto him, though He bear long with them? I tell you He will avenge them speedily. Nevertheless when the Son of Man cometh, shall He find faith on the earth?* (Luke 18:1-8).

The judge did not want to hear the woman's plea for justice, but the woman pressed him so hard and so long that he granted the woman's request. The judge did this not because he felt sorry for her or had compassion on her, but the judge granted her petition simply because the lady literally "got on his nerves." The widow, realizing the judge's reluctance and refusal to hear her, could have lost hope, lost faith, and simply given up. But the woman was persistent, and her persistence was actually fueled and empowered by her faith, a faith that declares, "I don't care how long it takes; I don't care what I have to suffer or what pain I must endure; I don't care who doesn't agree with me or doesn't like me for believing God; I know that if I keep on keeping on, one day, sooner or later, my change is going to come and I will see the salvation of the Lord."

POWER

My change is going to come and I will see the salvation of the Lord.

LIVING

Regardless of the excesses and some erroneous teachings that have been associated with the "Word of Faith" and Charismatic movements, Christians must forever remember and be mindful of the fact that the Word of God declares that anything in our lives that is not rooted in or brought about by faith in the Almighty, is sin. For without faith it is impossible to please God. The just (righteous men and women of God) shall and must live by faith. Faith for the believer is what gasoline is for an automobile; it's what electricity is for lights and high-powered appliances. It (faith in God and confidence in self) is what fuels our lives and gives motivation, inspiration, and eternal hope for our existence.

As the motivational and inspirational speaker Les Brown says about faith in God and in self:

> Within you lies the power to seize the hour and live your dreams. Faith is the oil that takes the friction out of living. Faith will enable you to turn liabilities into assets and stumbling blocks into stepping stones. When you begin to have faith, your load will get heavy but your knees won't buckle, you'll get knocked down but you won't get knocked out. You've got to have faith if you are going to make it in life. You must believe in yourself and in a power greater than yourself, and do your best and don't worry about the rest. You must maintain faith and work as if everything depended on you, and pray as if everything depended on God.

Please, let me be clear on what faith is, so that you make no mistakes about what I'm talking about. I'm not talking about some kind of feel-good confession rooted in humanism, saying, "I'm OK, you're OK." Nor am I referring to some kind of manipulation of Scripture to formulate my recipe for success. That's a form of Charismatic witchcraft, and I don't associate with witches.

No! When I say, "faith," I'm talking about complete, absolute, uncompromising trust in God. It is a faith that knows my successes in life are not because of some great wonderful ability of my own, but because my help comes from the Lord (see Ps. 40:17). For He, the Lord God Almighty, enables me to do His good will and all things for His good pleasure (see Phil. 2:13).

POWER

Faith in God and confidence in self fuels our lives and gives motivation, inspiration, and eternal hope.

It is God who works all things together and does all things for our good. In accordance with His calling on our lives and His overall purpose for humankind, He does these things (trials as well as blessings) to develop and reveal our love for Him. Love directed toward God is reflected and expressed by our obedience to His Word and submission to His commands (see 1 John 5:2-3). We must know that the supreme principle of faith—*"Faith... worketh by love"* (Gal. 5:6)—is the product of God's love toward us.

Often, we trust only those people who love us, the ones we are sure have our best interest at heart. With agape love, the recipient's welfare is always the giver's number one concern. Knowing this makes it easier to trust the heavenly Father, the One who loved you while you were yet a sinner, unworthy of love. Having promised that He will never leave or forsake us, no matter how difficult the circumstances, or how severe the situation, we are not without hope. Our hope makes us not ashamed *"because the love of God is shed abroad in our hearts by the Holy Ghost which is given unto us"* (Rom. 5:5). Faith worketh by love.

Patience and Waiting on God

The problem with most Christians is that we are far too impatient. If God doesn't speak in the first five minutes of our prayer time, we get up, shake ourselves off, and concede that God is not talking today. We no longer have the same tenacity, diligence, and persistence as the saints of old. Those saints of bygone days would get on their faces before God and grab hold of the horns of the altar and refuse to let go until they received a sure word from God. Unlike those precious men and women of God, we have become the "microwave" generation. We want everything overnight, even Christian maturity. We want whatever is quick, fast, and in a hurry. We've deleted, erased, and totally obliterated from our Bibles and our thoughts those passages of Scripture that command us to wait on God during turbulent, troubling, and unsure times.

> *My brethren, count it all joy when ye fall into divers temptations; knowing this, that the trying of your faith worketh patience. But let patience have her perfect work, that ye may be perfect and entire, wanting nothing* (James 1:2-4).

You might ask me, "Bishop, why (there's that *why* again) does it often take God so long to answer our prayers?" We put a petition, request, or question before God on a Monday, and it might be the next week or next month before God gives a reply.

This tests our faith to see if we will continue to serve God, even if He delays His reply. If God decides to prolong an answer or provision for our needs, are we willing and secure enough in His sovereignty to trust and wait on Him, regardless of how bleak the situation may look? My brothers and sisters, we have to let patience have its perfect (complete, absolute, to full maturity) work.

God's reply to the nagging questions and complex issues

that preoccupy our thoughts is, "I may not answer you right away, but go ahead and question why, and wait on Me."

> *But they that wait upon the Lord shall renew their strength; they shall mount up with wings as eagles; they shall run, and not be weary; and they shall walk, and not faint* (Isaiah 40:31).

What are you waiting for? I'm waiting for an answer. Does your vision tarry? Wait for it. Be diligent. Don't become weary in well doing: for in due season you shall reap the reward of your request, your petition, your labor, and the answers to your "whys," if you faint not (see Gal. 6:9).

Has God told you that He has destined you for a certain thing? Has God given you a vision of ministry? Has He promised you a particular blessing? Maybe you're single and God has assured you that you'll be married at an appointed time. But it seems as if the mate that God has fitted for your specific needs is nowhere in sight.

There are no manuals that instruct us step by step as to the proper way to seek the Lord. Like lovemaking, the pursuit is spontaneous and individually conceived out of the power of the moment. Some seek Him quietly, with soft tears falling quietly down a weary face. Others seek Him while walking the sandy beaches of a cove, gazing into the swelling currents of an evening tide. Some would raise their hands and praise and adore Him with loving expressions of adoration. There are no rules—just that we seek Him with our whole hearts.

We are like blind people when it comes to spiritual issues; we are limited. However, we should be challenged by our limitations. When there is a strong desire, we overcome our inabilities and press our way into His presence.

My friend, don't be afraid to stretch out your hands to reach after Him. Cry after Him. Whatever you do, do not allow this moment to pass you by!

If any of these predicaments are your present experience, I remind you of what God told His prophet Habakkuk. At a time when the prophet was despondent because of what he had seen and experienced, God said, *"Write the vision, and make it plain upon tables, that he* [you] *may run that readeth it* [to pursue it and fulfill it]. *For the vision is yet for an appointed time, but at the end it shall speak, and not lie: though it tarry, wait for it; because it will surely come, it will not tarry* [delay]" (Hab. 2:2-3).

POWER

Seek and you will find God.

LIVING

If God has spoken to you about your life and has shown you a glorious end to the matter, wait on it. If, in your waiting, you exercise faith, prayer, and patience, the vision shall surely come to pass. The Lord your God is not a man that He should lie nor the son of man that He should repent (see Num. 23:19). God says:

> *I know the thoughts that I think toward you . . . thoughts of peace, and not of evil, to give you an expected end. Then shall ye call upon me, and ye shall go and pray unto me, and I will hearken unto you. And ye shall seek me, and find me, when ye shall search for me with all your heart. And I will be found of*

> *you . . . and I will turn away your captivity . . .* (Jeremiah 29:11-14a).

TRIBULATION WORKS PATIENCE

> *Therefore being justified by faith, we have peace with God through our Lord Jesus Christ: by whom also we have access by faith into this grace wherein we stand, and rejoice in hope of the glory of God. And not only so, but we glory in tribulations also: knowing that tribulation worketh patience* (Romans 5:1-3).

Patience, contrary to popular belief, is not the same as waiting. Waiting is a passive posture, but patience is an active principle. Waiting, by itself, is by no means a guarantee of receiving the promise God has for your life. If that were the case, the five virgins caught without oil in their lamps would have been ready at the Lord's coming. (See Matthew 25.)

Also, the Hebrews who came out of Egypt would have entered the Promised Land. No! Patience is not just "waiting on God." Patience is based on the scriptural principle of persistence and perseverance (steadfastness in delay). Patience also does not come by prayer alone. As a matter of fact, a prayer for patience is only an acknowledgment of your lack of it and does not mean God will grant your request through a supernatural gift. No! My brother and sister, I wish it were that easy. As a matter of fact, when you ask God for patience, you only get it as a by-product of something else that the Lord sends your way. Are you curious to know what that something else is? (I know you are!) It is tribulation.

POWER

Patience is not the same as waiting.

LIVING

Tribulation. There is absolutely no other God-given way to grow in the fruit of patience. Trib-u-la-tion. The word even sounds funny and undesirable, but it's a necessary element of Christian perfection and a primary prerequisite in receiving the promises of God.

Tribulation. What is it? What does it mean? Is it affliction? Does it mean I'm going to have to suffer? Yes!

Tribulation means all of these and many other undesirable and unwelcome things that I will discuss in a later chapter. But without exercising patience, we will not be able to receive the full counsel of the Lord, nor will we see the vision of God come to pass in our lives. There will be no patience without tribulation.

Many times we pray for things, but we don't recognize or understand the answer to our prayers. Remember, in all things God has a divine process and order by which He operates everything on the earth.

POWER

The genius of success is to be able to see the good that hides in every situation.

LIVING

We ask for strength, and God sends us difficult situations to make us strong. We pray for wisdom, and God provides us with problems that provoke us to come up with solutions and develop wisdom. We ask for prosperity, and God gives us strength to work and wisdom to invent. We ask for favor, and God gives us responsibility. A large percentage of our success is the result of our eating the bread of adversity and drinking the bitter waters of affliction.

The genius of success is to be able to see the good that hides in every situation. As a pessimist sees obstacles in his opportunities, so an optimist sees opportunities in his obstacles. Tribulation works patience.

SEEKING GOD TAKES FOCUS

Seeking God also takes focus. This search has to be what the police call an A.P.B.—an "all points bulletin." All of the department is asked to seek the same thing. Thus our search can't be a distracted, half-hearted curiosity. There must be something to produce a unified effort to seek God. Body, soul, and spirit—all points—seeking the same thing.

There is a blessing waiting for us. It will require an A.P.B. to bring it into existence, but it will be worth attaining. Who knows what God will release if we go on an all-out God-hunt.

I believe there are times when we grow weary of human answers. The crucial times that arise in our lives require more than good advice. We need a word from God. There are moments when we need total seclusion. We come home from work, take the telephone receiver off the hook, close the blinds, and lie before God for a closer connection. In Job's case, he was going through an absolute crisis. His finances were obliterated. His cattle, donkeys, and oxen were destroyed. His crops were gone. In those days it would be comparable to the crash of the stock market. It was as if Job, the richest man, had gone bankrupt. What a shock to his system to realize that all are vulnerable. It is sobering to realize that one incident, or a sequence of events, can radically alter our lifestyles.

Unfortunately, it generally takes devastation on a business level to make most men commit more of their interest to relationships. Job probably could have reached out to his children for comfort, but he had lost them, too. His marriage had deteriorated to the degree that Job said his wife abhorred his breath (see Job 19:17). Then he also became ill. Have you ever gone through a time in your life when you felt you had been jinxed? Everything that could go wrong, did! Frustration turns into alienation. So now what? Will you use this moment to seek God or to brood over your misfortune? With the right answer, you could turn the jail into a church!

> *Seek ye the Lord while He may be found, call ye upon Him while He is near: Let the wicked forsake his way, and the unrighteous man his thoughts: and let him return unto the Lord, and He will have mercy upon him; and to our God, for He will abundantly pardon* (Isaiah 55:6-7).

Job said, *"Behold, I go forward, but He is not there"* (Job 23:8a). It is terrifying when you see no change coming in the future. Comfort comes when you know that the present adversity will soon be over. But what comfort can be found when it seems as though the problem will never cease? Job said, "I see no help, no sign of God, in the future." It actually is satan's trick to make you think help is not coming. That hopelessness then produces anxiety. On the other hand, sometimes the feeling that you eventually will come to a point of transition can give you the tenacity to persevere in the current challenge. But there often seems to be no slackening in distress. Like a rainstorm that will not cease, the waters of discouragement begin to fill the tossing ship with water. Suddenly you experience a sinking feeling. However, there is no way to sink a ship when you do not allow the waters from the outside to get on the inside! If the storms keep coming, the lightning continues to flash, and the thunder thumps on through the night, what matters is keeping the waters out of the inside. Keep that stuff out of your spirit!

Like a desperate sailor trying to plug a leaking ship, Job frantically cast back and forth in his mind, looking for some shred, some fragment of hope, to plug his leaking ship. Exasperated, he sullenly sat in the stupor of his condition and sadly confessed, "I go forward, but He is not there. I can't find Him where I thought He would be."

Have you ever told yourself that the storm would be over soon? And the sun came and the sun left, and still the same rains beat vehemently against the ship. It almost feels as if God missed His appointment. You thought He would move by now! Glancing nervously at your watch you think, *Where is He!* Remember, dear friend, God doesn't synchronize His timing by your little mortal clock. He has a set time to bless you; just hold on.

> *For the vision is yet for an appointed time,*
> *but at the end it shall speak, and not lie:*

> *though it tarry, wait for it; because it will surely come, it will not tarry* (Habakkuk 2:3).

Someone once said that studying the past prepares us for the future. It is important to look backward and see the patterns that cause us to feel some sense of continuity. But Job said, "Looking back, I could not perceive Him" (see Job 23:8b). "Why did I have to go through all of this? Is there any reason why I had to have this struggle?" Quite honestly, there are moments when life feels like it has all the purpose of gross insanity. Like a small child cutting paper on the floor, there seems to be no real plan, only actions. These are the times that try men's hearts. These are the times when we seek answers! Sometimes, even more than change, we need answers! "God, if You don't fix it, please, please explain it!"

We are reasoning people; we need to know why. Isn't that need one of the primary characteristics separating us from animals and lesser forms of life? We are reasoning, resourceful creatures. We seek answers. Yet there are times that, even after thorough evaluation, we cannot find our way out of the maze of happenstance!

POWER POINTS FOR LIVING

1. God's truth transforms. Have you been transformed since hearing God's truth? How?

2. The supreme principle of faith is the product of God's love toward us. What is the connection between faith and love?

3. They who wait on the Lord will renew their strength. Do you feel tired, stressed, worn out? Wait on the Lord—settle into His presence and feel your strength energize you!

4. Seek Him; and when you search for Him with all your heart, you will find Him. Write about a time when you found God waiting for you to find Him.

5. Without exercising patience we will not receive the full counsel of the Lord. Why is it so hard to have patience?

6. Patience is not the same as waiting. What is the difference?

7. The genius of success is to see the good that hides in every situation. Is it sometimes hard for you to see good in situations and circumstances? How is trust in God the answer?

CHAPTER 4

SPIRIT POWER

Any teacher will tell you that education begins not with lectures or speeches, but with interaction with the pupil. The classes are not really successful until the teacher has sufficiently stimulated the students to the point where they begin to ask questions about the subject being studied. With hands raised, they ask the teacher, "Why?" Then the explanation process begins. Before you know it, you have a serious dialogue going on, all centered on the inquisition: *why?*

As the teacher explains, she establishes a relationship with the student. The teacher knows she has the student in the palms of her hands. If she can get you to ask a question, she has motivated you. When you ask why, you're saying, "I'm interested in what you're teaching." At that precise moment, the teacher has engaged you (the student) not only in the education process, but in the actual learning experience.

Teachers who successfully educate not only must establish and maintain a dialogue with the students; they must also adequately and competently answer complex, difficult, and perplexing questions in the minds of students. From that point, the interaction between students and teacher conveys the message that says, "I respect your ability as a teacher to be able to give me answers." At this stage in the educational process, trust begins. If the teacher has proven continually that he or she has the students' personal as well as academic interests in mind, the learning process advances to the pivotal and most warranted stage referred to as discipleship.

From that point on, the student communicates to the teacher that what he wants to gain through their relationship is an exchange. Not only an exchange of answers, but for the teacher to teach him how to reason like a teacher. Therefore, this exchange will enable the student to become a teacher and ultimately teach other people. This is what God really desires and wishes to share with us as disciples of Christ.

God wants all of His children to have intimate dialogue with Him.

God desires all His children to have intimate dialogue with Him, like He had with Adam and Eve before the Fall. God, our heavenly Father, still seeks to walk with us in the cool of the day. Contrary to erroneous beliefs, God has always sought to communicate with His most blessed and highest earthly creation—humankind. God wants to communicate with us, which is one of the primary reasons He sent the Holy Spirit to commune with us—so we might learn something of His ways and purposes. The Scripture declares that "...ye need not that any man teach you: but as the same anointing teacheth you of all things, and is truth, and is no lie, and even as it hath taught you, ye shall abide in him" (1 John 2:27).

Just as college professors relate to students, God, by His Spirit, wants to have the same exchange with us. God's desire is to be with us, to work with us, to shape and mold us, to convene and plan with us, and to deal with us until we get to the point that we grow up from being students and become teachers ourselves.

> *That we henceforth be no more children, tossed to and fro, and carried about with every wind of doctrine, by the sleight of men, and cunning craftiness, whereby they lie in wait to deceive. But speaking the truth in love, may grow up into him in all things, which is the head, even Christ* (Ephesians 4:14-15).

Teachers impart wisdom to potential students and wisdom one to another, thus the *School of the Spirit.*

Teacher's Pet

There's no way that you can be the kind of student who

goes into overtime and not become the teacher's pet. Remember seeing them in school? They were those students who always were in the teacher's face, and the teacher just loved them. They always asked why, as if everything the teacher discussed was so interesting. You were probably like me, always so bored and so sick of them, you wanted to hit them in the head with an apple. They just kept asking why, and the teacher seemed to enjoy them so much. They had established that teacher-to-student, student-to-teacher relationship. God says, "Don't sit in My class and be reluctant to ask questions. I'm the Master Teacher, the Good Master Teacher." If you really want to get something going with Me, start draining from the milk of My wisdom, start pulling from Me.

> *Ask, and it shall be given you; seek, and ye shall find; knock, and it shall be opened unto you* (Matthew 7:7).

God wants us to be inquisitive. He's tired of His children being passive and accepting everything that comes into their lives. He wants us to question Him that we may find clarity and find effective solutions to the problems confronting us day in and day out. He wants you to take a stand and start asking, "Why?" He's tired of us lying down and saying, "This is the way it's got to be. I don't think there's any way it's going to change." God said, "I want you to contest Me, and ask, 'Why?'"

POWER

If you really want to know, ask Me.

LIVING

PETER, THE MASTER TEACHER'S PET

The earthly ministry of Jesus began with His teaching, training, developing, and mentoring of 12 men. The Bible refers to them as disciples. The word *disciple* comes from the Greek word *mathetes*, which means "a learner or student."

It was the tradition of Jesus' day that disciples not only learned from the teacher's lectures and discourses, but also by observing and experiencing every aspect of the teacher's very life. Likewise, the 12 disciples literally lived with the Teacher. They actually watched everything the Teacher did. The disciples listened to everything the Teacher said. They ate with Him and traveled with Him. The disciples were in close proximity with each and every personal aspect of Jesus' (the Master Teacher's) life.

The Church exists today as a result of the obedience and faithfulness of those 12 men, minus one (Judas). It is quite evident that Jesus was an enormously good, proficient, and effective Teacher who prepared 11 of His 12 men to go on and change the entire world and course of all humankind. No other teacher, school, or university can claim such success and effectiveness.

However, out of the 12 men, one stood out above all the rest. It was Peter. He later became known as the apostle Peter, the one Jesus called a rock. A very unique and passionate quality about this disciple distinguished him from the other 11. That quality was Peter's dogged determination to understand issues. He was known for always asking *why*.

POWER

Jesus was an enormously good, proficient, and effective Teacher.

LIVING

No doubt the other disciples thought Peter was a big mouth. They probably said he talked too much. They probably felt that Peter thought he was a know-it-all, but it was Peter's tendency to always ask "why" that caused Jesus, the Teacher, to notice this loudmouthed man and reward him with the much-desired position of Teacher's pet. Notice, I said reward and not appoint.

You may be appointed to be a disciple but you have to

earn the right—through diligence to know truth—to be the Teacher's pet. That's why Jesus chose Peter. Jesus knew that if enough of Peter's "whys" were answered, then the loud-mouthed, nosey, obnoxious fisherman would eventually become a great leader and apostle whom God could use to get the world's attention.

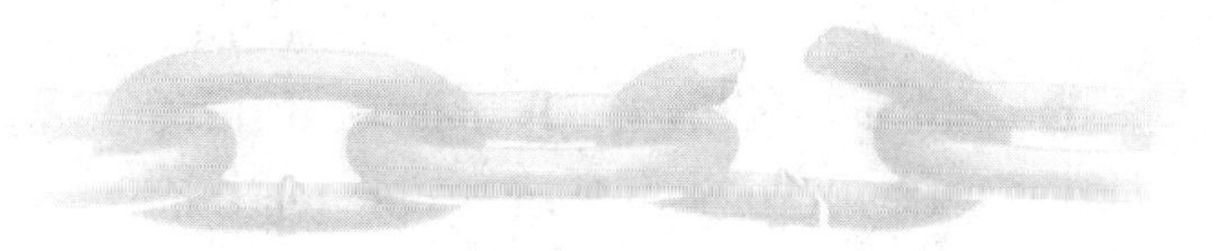

I love to surround myself with people who can stir up the fire in me. Some people in the Body of Christ know just what to say to ignite the very fire in you. However, no one can ignite in you what you do not possess! If the cold winds of opposition have banked the fire and your dream is dying down, I challenge you to rekindle your desire to achieve whatever God has called you to do. Don't lose your fire. You need that continued spark for excellence to overcome all the blight of being ostracized.

Fire manifests itself in two ways. First, it gives light. Whenever you maintain your fire, it produces the light of optimism against the blackness of crises and critics alike. As long as you maintain that fire-like attitude, you will find a way to survive the struggle. A man never dies with a twinkle in his eyes. Second, fire gives heat. Heat can't be seen, but it can be felt. When you are burning with the passion to survive, the heat can be felt. Invisible but effective, your intensity is always detected in your speech and attitude.

Every man and woman of God must also remember that fire needs fuel. Feed the fire. Feed it with the words of people who motivate you. Feed it with vision and purpose. When stress comes, fan the flames. Gather the wood. Pour gasoline on it if you have to, but don't let it die!

God is no respecter of persons. He does not grant favor or special privileges based on human ability or earthly accomplishments. God does show favor to those who hunger and thirst for righteousness. God favors those who thirst to know the truth and desire, no matter how great the cost, to do the will of God. It is evident that Jesus gave more attention to the development of three of the disciples—Peter, James, and John. But there was something extra significant about the relationship between Jesus and Peter, and that's what was so significant, the fact that they had a relationship.

Through Peter's persistence in asking questions, he initiated an exchange that developed a relationship between student and Teacher. It caused the Teacher to spend special time with the student. Every time something sacred and significant happened in Jesus' life and ministry, Peter was there. When Moses and Elijah appeared on the Mount of Transfiguration, who was there? Peter. When Jesus raised the little girl from the dead, He put everybody, including the family, out of the room, except for three of His disciples. Who was one of those disciples? Yes, you guessed it, Peter! Everywhere and every time something exciting was going on in Jesus' life and ministry, Simon Peter was there.

Become the Teacher's pet!

LIVING

Why would God spend special time with one student or child of God in comparison to another child of God? Isn't that showing partiality? Doesn't God love all His children just the same? The answer to that question is yes, God does love all His children with the same degree of love. But God is a wise businessman as well as sovereign Lord. He spends extra time, not based upon His loving one more than another, but because the Father God knows, as well as Jesus, that you invest more time in individuals who exhibit a greater desire to know the truth, operate in those truths, and wish to influence and persuade others with that truth.

God desires for us to know His will more than we want to know it. If we are willing to ask God why and let Him transform us into receiving His will, God will show us His favor and answer the "whys" of every asking heart.

POWER POINTS FOR LIVING

1. God desires all His children to have intimate dialogue with Him. Do you take the time to dialogue with God? Why—or why not?

2. God says, "If you really want to know Me, ask Me!" What question is at the top of your list to ask God?

3. God is tired of His children being passive and accepting everything that comes into their lives. In what areas of your life can you be more assertive and questioning? (At work? School? In relationships?)

4. You may be appointed to be a disciple, but you have to earn the right—through diligence to know truth—to be the Teacher's pet. Do you have a desire to be the Teacher's pet?

5. God does not grant favor or special privileges based on human ability or earthly accomplishments. How can you gain God's favor?

6. God invests more time in individuals who exhibit a greater desire to know the truth, operate in those truths, and wish to influence and persuade others with that truth. List three ways you can exhibit a greater desire to know the truth.

7. God will answer the "whys" of our hearts. List three "whys" of your heart.

CHAPTER 5

POWER AND COMPASSION

And they brought young children to Him, that He should touch them: and His disciples rebuked those that brought them. But when Jesus saw it, He was much displeased, and said unto them, Suffer the little children to come unto Me, and forbid them not: for of such is the kingdom of God. Verily I say unto you, Whosoever shall not receive the kingdom of God as a little child, he shall not enter therein. And He took them up in His arms, put His hands upon them, and blessed them (Mark 10:13-16).

It is interesting to me that just before the incident in Mark 10 took place, the Lord was ministering on the subject of divorce and adultery. When He brought up that subject, someone brought the children to Him so He could touch them. Broken homes often produce broken children. These little ones are often caught in the crossfire of angry parents. It reminds me of a newscast report on the Gulf War. It was a listing of the many young men who were accidentally killed by their own military—killed, however innocently, in the confusion of the battle. The newscaster called it "friendly fire." I thought, *What is friendly about bleeding to death with your face buried in the hot sand of a strange country? I mean, it doesn't help much when I am dead!* Many children are wounded in the friendly fire of angry parents.

POWER

There is power in compassion.

LIVING

Who were these nameless persons who had the insight and the wisdom to bring the children to the Master? They brought the children to Him that He might touch them. What a strange interruption to a discourse on adultery and divorce. Here are these little children dragging dirty blankets and blank gazes into the presence of a God who is dealing with grown-up problems. He takes time from His busy schedule not so much to counsel them, but just to touch them. That's all it takes. There is power in compassion.

I salute all the wonderful people who work with children. Whether through children's church or public school, you have a very high calling. Don't forget to touch their little lives with a word of hope and a smile of encouragement. It may be the only one some will receive. You are the builders of our future. Be careful, for you may be building a house that we will have to live in! Encourage the future. Share a smile with a child.

What is wrong with these disciples that they became angry at some nameless person who aimed these little arrows at the only answer they might ever have gotten to see? Who told them they were too busy to heal their own children? Jesus stopped teaching on the cause of divorce and marital abuse to touch the victim, to minister to the effect of the abuse. He told them to suffer the little children to come. Suffer the suffering to come! It is hard to work with hurting people, but the time has come for us to suffer the suffering to come. Anything, whether an injured animal or a hospital patient—if it is hurt, it is unhappy.

We cannot get a wounded lion to jump through hoops! Hurting children as well as hurting adults can carry the unpleasant aroma of bitterness. In spite of the challenge, it is foolish to give up on your own. So they brought the "ouch" to the Band-Aid, and He stopped His message for His mission. Imagine tiny hands outstretched, little faces upturned, perching like sparrows on His knee. They came to get a touch, but He always gives us more than we expect. He held them with His loving arms. He touched with His sensitive hands. But most of all, He blessed them with His compassionate heart!

COMPASSION

I am concerned that we maintain our compassion. How can we be in the presence of a loving God and then not love little ones? When Jesus blessed the children, He challenged the adults to become as children. Oh, to be a child again, to allow ourselves the kind of relationship with God that we may have missed as a child. Sometimes we need to allow the Lord to adjust the damaged places of our past. I am glad to say that God provides arms that allow grown children to climb up like little children and be nurtured through the tragedies of their early days. Isn't it nice to toddle into the presence of God and let Him hold you in His arms?

POWER

It is so important that we learn how to worship and adore Him, for in both is power for living.

LIVING

In God, we can become children again. Salvation is God giving us a chance to start over. He will not abuse the children that come to Him. Through praise, I approach Him like a toddler on unskillful legs. In worship, I kiss His face and am held by the caress of His anointing. He has no ulterior motive, for His caress is safe and wholesome. It is so important that we learn how to worship and adore Him, for in both is power for living. There is no better way to climb into His arms. Even if you were exposed to grown-up situations when you were a child, God can reverse what you've been through. He'll let the grown-up person experience the joy of being a child in His presence!

> *Then I passed by and saw you kicking about in your blood, and as you lay there in your blood I said to you, "Live!" I made you grow like a plant of the field. You grew up and developed and became the most beautiful of jewels. Your breasts were formed and your hair grew, you who were naked and bare. Later I passed by, and when I looked at you and saw that you were old enough for love, I spread the corner of my garment over you and covered your nakedness. I gave you My solemn oath and entered into a covenant with you, declares the Sovereign Lord, and you became Mine. I bathed you with water and washed the blood from you and put ointments on you. I clothed you with an embroidered dress and put leather sandals on you. I dressed you in fine linen and covered you with costly garments* (Ezekiel 16:6-10 NIV).

Reach out and embrace the fact that God has been watching over you all of your life. He covers you, He clothes you, and He blesses you! Rejoice in Him in spite of the broken places. God's grace is sufficient for your needs and your scars. He will anoint you with oil. The anointing of the Lord be upon you now! May it bathe, heal, and strengthen you as never before.

POWER

The anointing of God restores us and allows us to accomplish great and noble things. Believe it!

LIVING

If great things came from those who never suffered, we might think that they accomplished those things of their own accord. When a broken person submits to God, God gets the glory for the wonderful things He accomplishes—no matter how far that person has fallen. The anointing of God restores us and allows us to accomplish great and noble things. Believe it!

The hidden Christ that's been locked up behind your fears, your problems, and your insecurity, will come forth in your life. You will see the power of the Lord Jesus do a mighty thing.

And Mary said, Behold the handmaid of the Lord; be it unto me according to thy word.

> *And the angel departed from her* (Luke 1:38).

"Be it unto me according to thy word." Not according to my marital status. Not according to my job. Not according to what I deserve. "Be it unto me according to thy word."

ATTITUDES

Attitudes affect the way we live our lives. A good attitude can bring success. A poor attitude can bring destruction. An attitude results from perspective. I'm sure you understand what perspective is. Everyone seems to have a different perspective. It comes from the way we look at life, and the way we look at life is often determined by our history.

The events of the past can cause us to have an outlook or perspective on life that is less than God's perspective. The little girl who was abused learns to defend herself by not trusting men. This attitude of defensiveness often stretches into adulthood. If we have protected ourselves a certain way in the past with some measure of success, then it is natural to continue that pattern throughout life. Unfortunately, we often need to learn how to look past our perspective and change our attitudes.

The infirm woman whom Jesus healed was made completely well by His touch (see Luke 13:11-13). She couldn't help herself no matter how hard she tried, but Jesus unleashed her. He lifted a heavy burden from her shoulders and set her free. Jesus sets us free.

POWER

Look past your perspective and change your attitude.

LIVING

Today, many of us have things we need to be separated from or burdens we need lifted. We will not function effectively until those things are lifted off of us. We can function to a certain point under a load, but we can't function as effectively as we would if the thing were lifted off of us. Perhaps some of you right now have things that are weighing you down.

You need to commend yourself for having the strength to function under pressure. Unfortunately, we often bear the weight of it alone, since we don't feel free to tell anyone about our struggles. So whatever strides you have made, be they large or small, you have made them against the current.

It is God's intention that we be set free from the loads we carry. Many people live in codependent relationships. Others are anesthetized to their problems because they have had them so long. Perhaps you have become so accustomed to having a problem that even when you get a chance to be delivered, you find it hard to let it go. Problems can become like a security blanket.

POWER

Commend yourself for having the strength to function under pressure—then overcome the problem with His power.

LIVING

No Excuse

Jesus took away the woman's excuse. He said, *"Woman, thou art loosed from thine infirmity"* (Luke 13:12). The moment He said that, it required something of her that she hadn't had to deal with before. For 18 years she could excuse herself because she was handicapped. The moment He told her the problem was gone, she had no excuse.

Before you get out of trouble, you need to straighten out your attitude. Until your attitude is corrected, your trouble can't be corrected.

Why should we put up all the ramps and rails for the handicapped if we can heal them? You want everyone to make an allowance for your problem, but your problem needs to make an allowance for God and to humble itself to the point where you don't need special help. I'm not referring to physical handicaps; I'm addressing the emotional baggage that keeps us from total health. You cannot expect the whole human race to move over because you had a bad childhood. They will not do it. So you will end up in depression and frustration, and even confusion. You may have trouble with relationships because people don't accommodate your hang-up.

POWER

Christ wants to separate you from the source of your bitterness until it no longer gives you the kind of attitude that makes you a carrier of pain.

LIVING

One woman I pastored was extremely obnoxious. It troubled me deeply, so I took the matter to God in prayer. The Lord allowed me to meet her husband. When I saw how nasty he talked to her, I understood why, when she reached down into her reservoir, all she had was hostility. That's all she had taken in. You cannot give out something that you haven't taken in.

Christ wants to separate you from the source of your bitterness until it no longer gives you the kind of attitude that makes you a carrier of pain. Your attitude affects your situation—your attitude, not other people's attitude about you. Your attitude will give you life or death.

One of the greatest deliverances people can ever experience in life is to have their attitude delivered. It doesn't do you any good to be delivered financially if your attitude doesn't change. I can give you $5,000, but if your attitude, your mental perspective, doesn't change, you will be broke in a week because you'll lose it again. The problem is not how much you have, it's what you do with what you have. If you can change your attitude, you might have only $50, but you'll take that $50 and learn how to get $5 million.

TOTAL HEALING

When God comes to heal, He wants to heal your emotions also. Sometimes all we pray about is our situation. We bring God our shopping list of desires. Fixing circumstances is not the answer. Healing attitudes set people free to receive wholeness.

The woman who was crippled for 18 years was delivered from her infirmity. The Bible says she was made straight and glorified God. She got a new attitude. However, the enemy still tried to defeat her by using the people around her. He does not want to let you find health and strength. He may send another circumstance that will pull you down in the same way if you don't change your attitude.

When you first read about this woman, you might have thought that the greatest deliverance was her physical deliverance. I want to point out another deliverance that was even greater. The Bible said that when the Lord laid His hand on her, she was made straight. That's physical deliverance. Then her attitude changed. She entered into praise and thanksgiving and worshiped the Lord. This woman began to leap and rejoice and magnify God and shout the victory like anybody who has been delivered from an 18-year infirmity should. While she was glorifying God over here, the enemy was stirring up strife over there (see Luke 13:14). She just kept on glorifying God. She didn't stop praising God to answer the accusers.

YOUR DEFENSE

The Lord is your defense. You do not have to defend yourself. When God has delivered you, do not stop what you're doing to answer your accusers. Continue to bless His name, because you do not want your attitude to become defensive. When you have been through difficult times, you cannot afford to play around with moods and attitudes. Depression and defensiveness may make you vulnerable to the devil.

This woman had to protect herself by entering into defensive praise. This was not just praise of thanksgiving, but defensive praise. Defensive praise is a strategy and a posture of war that says, "We will not allow our attitude to crumble and fall."

POWER

The Lord is your defense.

LIVING

When you get to the point that you quit defending yourself or attacking others, you open up a door for the Lord to fight for you.

When this woman began to bless God, she built walls around her own deliverance. She decided to keep the kind of attitude that enabled the deliverance of God to be maintained in her life. When you have been through surgery, you cannot afford to fool around with Band-Aids.

When you're in trouble, God will reach into the mess and pull you out. However, you must be strong enough not to let people drag you back into it. Once God unleashes you, don't let anyone trap you into some religious fight. Keep praising Him. For this woman, the more they criticized her, the more she was justified because she just stood there and kept believing God. God is trying to get you to a place of faith. He is trying to deliver you from an attitude of negatives.

POWER

When you're in trouble, God will reach into the mess and pull you out.

LIVING

When you have had problems for many years, you tend to expect problems. God must have healed this woman's emotions also because she kept praising Him instead of paying attention to the quarrel of the religious folks around her. She could have easily fallen into negative thinking. Instead, she praised God.

Can you imagine what would have happened if she had stopped glorifying God and started arguing? If an argument could have gotten through her doors, this whole scene would have ended in a fight. But she was thankful and determined to express her gratitude.

The Lord wants to speak a word of faith to you. He wants to set you free from every power that has kept you in bondage. In order for that to be received in your spirit, you must allow Him to come in and instill faith. The emotional walls that surround us have to come down.

Love is eternal. It is not limited by time. When you commit yourself to loving someone, you make that commitment to all the person is. You are who you are because of your history. For me, that means I love my wife and who she has become. But for me to love her effectively, she must allow me into her history.

Many couples in a relationship argue over relatively insignificant things. Often the reason these things are important is one or the other is reminded of a past event. How can one person love another if he or she doesn't know the other person's history?

The Church has become too narrow in its approach to attitude. We want to keep our attitudes to ourselves and simply take them to God. Although we certainly should take them to Him, we also need to learn to "*bear ye one another's burdens*" (Gal. 6:2a).

Thousands walk in fear. The Church can give strength to counter that fear. Thousands have built a wall around them because they do not trust anyone else. The Church can help its members learn to trust one another. Thousands are codependent and get their value from a relationship with another person. The Church can point to God's love as the source for self-worth. We are not valuable because we love God; we are valuable because He loves us.

Jesus took away the ability of the infirm woman to make excuses for herself and gave her the strength to maintain an attitude of gratitude and praise. The Church today is to be the kind of safe haven that does the same thing. Those who are wounded should be able to come and find strength in our praise.

POWER

Those who are wounded should be able to find strength in our praise.

LIVING

Gratitude and defensive praise are contagious. Once Jesus addressed the naysayers, the others (who saw what He had done on the day He healed the infirm woman) began to rejoice (see Luke 13:17). The Church also must find room to join in praise when the broken are healed. Those who missed the great blessing that day were those who decided to argue about religion.

The Bible describes Heaven as a place where the angels rejoice over one sinner who comes into the faith (see Luke 15:10). They rejoice because Jesus heals those who are broken. Likewise God's people are to rejoice because the brokenhearted and emotionally wounded come to Him.

Christ unleashed power in the infirm woman that day. He healed her body and gave her the strength of character to keep a proper attitude. The woman who is broken and wounded today will find power unleashed within her too when she responds to the call and brings her wounds to the Great Physician.

That No Flesh Shall Glory in His Sight

> *Brothers, think of what you were when you were called. Not many of you were wise by human standards; not many were influential; not many were of noble birth. But God chose the foolish things of the world to shame the wise; God chose the weak things of the world to shame the strong. He chose the lowly things of this world and the despised things—and the things that are not—to nullify the things that are, that no flesh should glory in His presence* (1 Corinthians 1:26-28 NIV; 1 Corinthians 1:29 KJV).

God doesn't seek to manifest His glory and glorious works through those whom the world perceives as great and wonderful. He boldly declares without apology or apprehension that "My ways are not your ways; my thoughts are higher than your thoughts" (see Isa. 55:8-9). When people seek individuals to do great and monumental things, they look for those who have great education, wealth, prestige, and honor; they seek people of great nobility.

But God selects those who are like bums. He chooses those whom the world has rejected; those who have been ostracized and alienated from family, friends, and peers; those who are constantly criticized. God takes them and makes them and infuses them with His power, revelation, and wisdom so that they can be wondrously educated in the things of God. This occurs so they can greatly change and affect the things of the world.

God considers those who are of no account, those nobody expects to be anything; those whose family, friends, and relatives have thrown away and given up on. God takes those who are fearful and don't believe in themselves and makes them men and women of greatness with wealth, prestige, and honor—mighty men and women of valor! These are men and women like Abraham, Joseph, Gideon, Jacob, Peter, Deborah, Ruth, Esther, Mary, William J. Seymour, Oral Roberts, Bishop Mason of the Church of God in Christ, Aimee Semple McPherson of the Foursquare Church, and Kathryn Kuhlman, just to name a few. Why does God do this? Why does God use the rejected and the despised?

It's a simple but profound answer: that He, God, would get all the glory and not man, "that no flesh should glory in his presence." For the Word of God says that "we have this treasure in earthen vessels, that the excellency of the power may be of God and not of us" (2 Cor. 4:7).

It is God and not you. God says, "When I bring you out, your critics will know it was Me. I'm going to wait until you fail; I'm going to wait until you lose confidence in yourself, your education, your job, your influential title, your résumés, your friends, your family, your doctrines, your creed, and your denominational affiliation. When you've lost hope in everything earthly and feel totally worthless and are in complete despair, then I'm going to stretch forth My right hand. I'm going to pick your feet up out of the miry clay. I'm going to place you on a rock to stay. When nobody else will praise Me, praise will continually be in your mouth, because you are going to know it was My right hand, and My holy arm that brought you victory. It was I who brought you out. It was I who gave you a breakthrough, and not yourself, nor the help of man."

God uses the rejected and despised!

LIVING

Do you still wonder why you have had to go through all the pain and hell you have been experiencing since getting serious with God and vowing to obey Him, no matter what the cost?

The reason: you would no longer place confidence in the flesh, for it is God who works in you both to will and to do

His good will and pleasure. But in all things we must give Him the praise, not man, *"that no flesh should glory in His presence"* (1 Cor. 1:29).

POWER POINTS FOR LIVING

1. Encourage the future, share a smile with a child. Do you see children as more of a bother than a blessing? Think of some ways you can reach out to children in your family, neighborhood, and church.

2. God's loving arms allow grown-ups to climb up into His lap like children and be nurtured through the tragedies of their early days. Write about tough times you may have had growing up. Allow God to comfort you and give you strength to forgive those who may have harmed you.

3. The anointing of God gives us power to accomplish great and noble things. Believe it! List a few "great and noble things" that you would like to accomplish in your lifetime. Think big and believe!

4. It is God's intention that we be set free from the loads we carry. Write three burdens that you can't seem to unload. Then hand them over to God—permanently.

5. Your attitude will give you life or death. Do people think you have a good or bad attitude about life? As a child of God, you need to project a good attitude—after all, your heavenly Father has given you a Kingdom inheritance!

6. Jesus heals us *totally*. Have you allowed Jesus to heal you—totally? If not—why not?

7. We are not valuable because we love God; we are valuable because He loves us. What are some ways you can thank Him for loving you and placing such high value on your life?

CHAPTER 6

VICTORIOUS POWER

Amnon was wicked. He brutally raped his sister Tamar. He destroyed her destiny and her future. He slashed her self-esteem. He spoiled her integrity. He broke her femininity like a twig under his feet. He assassinated her character. She went into his room a virgin with a future. When it was over, she was a bleeding, trembling, crying mass of pain.

This story from Second Samuel 13 is one of the saddest stories in the Bible. It also reveals what people can do to one another if left alone without God. For when Amnon and Tamar were left alone, he assassinated her. The body survived, but her femininity was destroyed. She felt as though she would never be the woman that she would have been had it not happened.

Have you ever had anything happen to you that changed you forever? Somehow, you were like a palm tree bending in the wind and you survived. Yet you knew you would never be the same. Perhaps you have spent every day since then bowed over. You could in no way lift up yourself. You shout. You sing. You skip. But when no one is looking, when the crowd is gone and the lights are out, you are still that trembling, crying, bleeding mass of pain that is abused, bowed, bent backward, and crippled.

Maybe you are in the Church, but you are in trouble. People move all around you, and you laugh, even entertain them. You are fun to be around. But they don't know. You can't seem to talk about what happened in your life.

POWER

Have you ever had anything happen to you that changed you forever?

LIVING

The Bible says Tamar was in trouble. The worst part about it is that, after Amnon had abused her, he didn't even want her. He had messed up her life and spoiled what she was proud of. He assassinated her future and damaged her prospects. Tamar said, "What you're doing to me now is worse than what you did to me at first." She said, "Raping me was horrible, but not wanting me is worse" (see 2 Sam. 13:16).

Maybe you have gone through divorces, tragedies, and adulterous relationships, and you've been left feeling unwanted. You can't shout over that sort of thing. You can't leap over that kind of wall. It injures something about you that changes how you relate to everyone else for the rest of your life. Amnon didn't even want Tamar afterward. She pleaded with him, "Don't throw me away." She was fighting for the last strands of her femininity. Amnon called a servant and said, "Throw her out." The Bible says he hated Tamar with a greater intensity than that with which he had loved her before (see 2 Sam. 13:15).

God knows that the Amnon in your life really does not love you. He's out to abuse you. The servant picked up Tamar, opened the door, and threw the victimized woman out. She lay on the ground outside the door with nowhere to go. He told the servant, "Lock the door."

What do you do when you are trapped in a transitory state, neither in nor out? You're left lying at the door, torn up and disturbed, trembling and intimidated. The Bible says she cried. Filled with regrets, pains, nightmare experiences, seemingly unable to find relief... unable to rise above it, she stayed on the ground. She cried.

She had a coat, a cape of many colors. It was a sign of her virginity and of her future. She was going to give it to her husband one day. She ripped it up, meaning, "I have no future. It wasn't just that he took my body. He took my future. He took my esteem and value away."

You may have been physically or emotionally raped and robbed. You survived, but you left a substantial degree of self-esteem in Amnon's bed. Have you lost the road map that directs you back to where you were before?

The Lord says, "I want you. I will give you power for living." No matter how many men like Amnon have told you, "I don't want you," God says, "I want you. I've seen you bent over. I've seen the aftereffects of what happened to you. I've seen you at your worst moment. I still want you."

God has not changed His mind. God loves with an everlasting love.

POWER

Have you lost the road map that directs you back to where you were before?

LIVING

INNER ASSURANCE

Normally, anytime there is a crash, there is an injury. If one person collides with another, they generally damage everything associated with them. In the same way, a crashing relationship affects everyone associated with it, whether it is in a corporate office, a ministry, or a family. That jarring and shaking does varying degrees of damage to everyone involved. Whether we like to admit it or not, we are affected by the actions of others to various degrees. The amount of the effect, though, depends on the nature of the relationship.

What is important is the fact that we don't have to die in the crashes and collisions of life. We must learn to live life with a seat belt in place, even though it is annoying to wear. Similarly, we need spiritual and emotional seat belts. We don't need the kind that harness us in and make us live like mannequins; rather, we need the kind that are invisible, but greatly appreciated in a crash.

Inner assurance is the seat belt that stops you from going through the roof when you are rejected. It is inner assurance that holds you in place. It is the assurance that God is in control and that what He has determined no one can disallow! If He said He was going to bless you, then disregard the mess and believe a God who cannot lie. The rubbish can be removed and the bruises can be healed. Just be sure that when the smoke clears, you are still standing. You are too important to the purpose of God to be destroyed by a situation that is only meant to give you character and direction. No matter how painful, devastated, or disappointed you may feel, you are still here. Praise God, for He will use the cornerstone developed through rejections and failed relationships to perfect what He has prepared!

Lift your voice above the screaming sirens and alarms of men whose hearts have panicked! Lift your eyes above the billowing smoke and spiraling emotions. Pull yourself up—it could have killed you, but it didn't. Announce to yourself, "I am alive. I can laugh. I can cry, and by God's grace, I can survive!"

When Jesus encountered the infirm woman of Luke chapter 13, He called out to her. There may have been many fine women present that day, but the Lord didn't call them forward. He reached around all of them and found that crippled woman in the back. He called forth the wounded, hurting woman with a past. He issued the Spirit's call to those whose value and self-esteem had been destroyed by the intrusion of vicious circumstances.

POWER

The Holy Spirit restores those whose value and self-esteem have been destroyed by the intrusion of vicious circumstances.

LIVING

The infirm woman must have thought, "He cares about me. He cares about me. I'm frayed and torn, but He cares about me. I have been through trouble. I have been through this trauma, but He wants to help me." Perhaps she thought no one would ever care about her again, but Jesus did. He had a plan.

She may have known that it would take a while for her life to be completely put back together. She had many things to overcome. She was handicapped. She was probably filled with insecurities. Yet Jesus still called her forth for His touch.

If you can identify with the feelings of this infirm woman, then know that He's waiting on you and that He wants to connect with you. He sees your struggling and He knows all about your pain. He knows what happened to you 18 years ago or ten years ago or even last week. With patience He waits for you, as the father waited for the prodigal son. Jesus says to the hurting and crippled, "I want relationship with you enough to wait for you to hobble your way back home."

POWER

God sees you struggling and He knows about your pain.

LIVING

When the infirm woman came to Jesus, He proclaimed her freedom. When He did, she stood erect for the first time in 18 years. When you come to Jesus, He will cause you to stand in His power, His anointing. You will know how important you are to Him. Part of your recovery is to learn how to stand up and live in the "now" of life instead of the "then" of yesterday.

All you need to do is allow His power and anointing to touch the hurting places. He will take care of the secrets. He touches the places where you've been assassinated. He knows the person you would have been, the person you should have been, the person you could have been. God heals and restores as you call out to Him.

POWER

Allow His power and anointing to touch the hurting places.

LIVING

The enemy wanted to change your destiny through a series of events, but God will restore you to wholeness as if the events had never happened. He's delivering you by the power of His Spirit—victorious power.

> *...Not by might, nor by power, but by My spirit, saith the Lord of hosts* (Zechariah 4:6).

The anointing power of the living God is reaching out to you. He calls you forth to set you free. When you reach out to Him and allow the Holy Spirit to have His way, His anointing is present to deliver you. Demons will tremble. Satan wants to keep you at the door, but never let you enter. He wants to keep you down, but now his power is broken in your life.

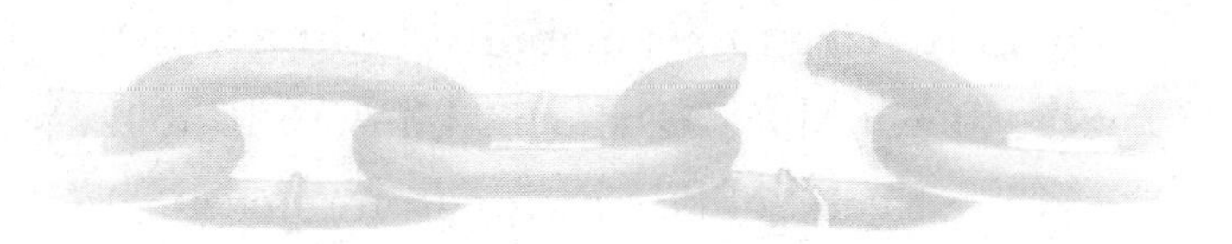

I can't help but wonder how much more we all would see of God if we would remove life's little buildups that clog the arteries of our hearts and keep us from seeing the glory of God. These are the obstacles that keep us seeking the wisdom of men rather than the wisdom of God! These are the obstacles that make us feel insecure while we wait for an answer. These are the obstacles that keep many well-meaning Christians needing prayer rather than giving prayer. In short, let's clean out our hearts and we will hear, worship, and experience God in a new dimension. Clean out every thought that hinders the peace and power of God.

> *Blessed are the pure in heart: for they shall see God* (Matthew 5:8).

This Scripture clearly draws a line of prerequisites necessary to see God in His fullest sense. He is often described as the invisible God (see Col. 1:15). God's invisibility doesn't refer to an inability to be seen as much as it does to your inability to behold Him. To the blind all things are invisible. How can I see this God who cannot be detected in my vision's periphery? Jesus taught that a pure heart could see God. No wonder David cried out, "Create in me a clean heart..." (Ps. 51:10).

The term used in Matthew 5:8 for "pure" comes from the Greek word *katharos*, which means "to clean out," much like a laxative. That may be funny, but it's true. Jesus is saying to give your heart a laxative when you've heard too much or seen too much. Don't carry around what God wants discarded. Give your heart a laxative and get rid of *"every weight, and the sin which doth so easily beset us"* (Heb. 12:1)! What God wants to unveil to you is worth the cleaning up to see.

Tamar knew the feeling of desertion. She understood that she was cast out. However, the Bible explains that Absalom took her in. You too may have been lying at the door. Perhaps you didn't have anywhere to go. You may have been half in and half out. You were broken and demented and disturbed. But God sent Absalom to restore you.

POWER

The anointing power of the living God is reaching out to you. He calls you forth to set you free.

LIVING

In this instance, Absalom depicts the purpose of real ministry. Thank God for the Church. It's the place where you can come broken and disgusted, and be healed, delivered, and set free in the name of Jesus.

Jesus said,

> *The Spirit of the Lord is upon Me, because He hath anointed Me to preach the gospel to the poor; He hath sent Me to heal the broken-hearted, to preach deliverance to the captives, and recovering of sight to the blind, to set at liberty them that are bruised* (Luke 4:18).

You may have thought that you would never rejoice again. God declares that you can have freedom in Him—

now! The joy that He brings can be restored to your soul. He identifies with your pain and suffering. He knows what it is like to suffer abuse at the hands of others. Yet He proclaims joy and strength. He will give you the garment of praise instead of the spirit of heaviness (see Isa. 61:3).

Once you have called out to Him, you can lift up your hands in praise. No matter what you have suffered, you can hold up your head. Regardless of who has hurt you, hold up your head!

> *Lift up your heads, O ye gates; even lift them up, ye everlasting doors; and the King of glory shall come in. Who is this King of glory? The Lord of hosts, He is the King of glory. Selah* (Psalms 24:9-10).

He will restore to you that which the cankerworm and the locust ate up (see Joel 2:25). He said, "I'm going to give it back to you."

Maybe you wrestle with guilt; He said:

> *Come now, and let us reason together, saith the Lord: though your sins be as scarlet, they shall be as white as snow; though they be red like crimson, they shall be as wool* (Isaiah 1:18).

All my life I have had a tremendous compassion for

hurting people. When other people would put their foot on them, I always tended to have a ministry of mercy. Perhaps it is because I've had my own pain. When you have suffered, it makes you able to relate to other people's pain. The Lord settled me in a ministry that tends to cater to hurting people. Sometimes when I minister, I find myself fighting back tears. Sometimes I can hear the cries of anguished people in the crowd.

Celebrate your victory and thank God you made it!

LIVING

Like Tamar, you're a survivor. You should celebrate your survival. Instead of agonizing over your tragedies, you should celebrate your victory and thank God you made it. I charge you to step over your adversity and walk into the newness. It is like stepping from a storm into the sunshine—step into it now.

Blessings

God has blessed me with two sons and two daughters. As a father, I have found that I have a ministry of hugs. When something happens, and I really can't fix it, I just hug them. I can't change how other people treated them. I can't change what happened at school. I can't make the teacher like them. I can't take away the insults. But I can hug them!

I believe the best nurses are the ones who have been patients. They have compassion for the victim. The Church needs to develop a ministry of hugs. The touch of the Master sets us free. The touch of a fellow pilgrim lets us know we are not alone in our plight.

The Holy Spirit is calling for the broken, infirm people to come to Jesus. He will restore and deliver. How do we come to Jesus? We come to His Body, the Church. It is in the Church that we can hear the Word of God. The Church gives us strength and nourishment. The Church is to be the place where we share our burdens and allow others to help us with them. The Spirit calls; the burdened need only heed the call.

Three Tenses of Faith

There are three tenses of faith! When Lazarus died, Martha, his sister, said, "Lord, if You would have been here, my brother would not have died." This is *historical* faith. Its view is digressive. Then when Jesus said, "Lazarus will live again," his sister replied, "I know he will live in the resurrection." This is *futuristic* faith. It is progressive. Martha says, "But *even now* You have the power to raise him up again." (See John 11:21-27.) I feel like Martha. Even now, after all you've been through, God has the power to raise you up again! This is the *present* tense of faith. Walk into your newness even now. You have been anointed with victorious power!

POWER POINTS FOR LIVING

1. The Lord says, "I want relationship with you. I will give you power for living." Is there anything holding you back from accepting God's power for living?

2. You can learn how to stand up and live in the "now" of life instead of the "then" of yesterday. What will your first step be?

3. God takes care of all the secrets. Think of your darkest secret. Now give it to God—and know that He already knew about it and had already forgiven you for it. Rejoice!

4. When you reach out to Him and allow the Holy Spirit to have His way, His anointing will deliver you. Do you believe this? Why, or why not?

5. Wear the garment of praise instead of the

spirit of heaviness. What wrappings do you need to discard that will allow you to praise your way into victory?

6. The Church gives us strength and nourishment. Do you attend church regularly? Why or why not?

7. Even now, after all you've been through, God has the power to raise you up again! Do you want to be raised up again, or are you comfortable in your familiar troubles and turmoil?

CHAPTER 7

POWER OVER FEAR

Have you ever tasted that cold, acid-like taste of fear? I mean the kind of fear that feels like a cinder block is being dragged across the pit of your stomach. It's the kind where cold chills trimmed with a prickly sensation flood your body, adorning itself in a distinct sense of nausea. No matter how strong we are, there is always something that can cause the heart to flutter and the pulse to weaken.

Fear is as lethal to us as paralysis of the brain. It makes our thoughts become arthritic and our memory sluggish. It is the kind of feeling that can make a graceful person stumble up the stairs in a crowd. You know what I mean—the thing that makes the articulate stutter and the rhythmic become spastic. Like an oversized growth, fear soon becomes impossible to camouflage. Telltale signs like trembling knees or quivering lips betray fear even in the most disciplined person. Fear is the nightmare of the stage; it haunts the hearts of the timid as well as of the intimidated.

From the football field to the ski slope, fear has a visa of entrance that allows it to access the most discriminating crowd. It is not prejudiced, nor is it socially conscious. It can attack the impoverished or the aristocratic. When it grips the heart of a preacher, his notes turn into a foreign language and his breathing becomes asthmatic.

To me, there is no fear like the fear of the innocent. This is the fear of a child who walks into a dark basement to find the light switch far from reach—and every mop and bucket becomes a sinister, sleazy creature whose cold breath lurks upon the neck of life's little apprentice. I can remember moments as a child when I thought my heart had turned into an African tom-tom that was being beaten by an insane musician whose determined beating would soon break through my chest like the bursting of a flood-engorged dam.

POWER

Fear is not prejudiced—
it attacks all.

LIVING

Even now I can only speculate how long it took for fear to give way to normalcy, or for the distant rumble of a racing heart to recede into the steadiness of practical thinking and rationality. I can't estimate time because fear traps time and holds it hostage in a prison of icy anxiety. Eventually, though, like the thawing of icicles on the roof of an aged and sagging house, my heart would gradually melt into a steady and less pronounced beat.

POWER

Fear traps time and holds it hostage in a prison of icy anxiety.

LIVING

I confess that maturity has chased away many of the ghosts and goblins of my youthful closet of fear. Nevertheless, there are still those occasional moments when reason gives way to the fanciful imagination of the fearful little boy in me, who peeks his head out of my now fully-developed frame the way a turtle sticks his head out of its shell with caution and precision.

LOVE OF THE FATHER

Thank God that He understands the hidden part within each of us. Paul's words from Galatians show how God understands the child in us, and He speaks to our blanket-clutching, thumb-sucking infantile need. In spite of our growth, income, education, or notoriety, He still speaks to the childhood issues of the aging heart. This is the ministry that only a Father can give.

Have you ever noticed that you are never a grown-up to

the ones who birthed you? They completely disregard the gray hairs, crows-feet, and bulging, blossoming waistlines of abundant life. No matter how many children call you Dad or Mom, to your parents you are still just a child yourself. They seem to think you have slipped into the closet to put on grown-up clothes and are really just playing a game. They must believe that somewhere beneath the receding hairline there is still a child, hiding in the darkness of adulthood. The worst part about it is (keep this quiet), I think they are right!

POWER

Beneath the receding hairline there is still a child, hiding in the darkness of adulthood.

LIVING

The Lord looks beyond our facades and sees the trembling places in our lives. He knows our innermost needs. No matter how spiritually mature we try to appear, He is still aware that lurking in the shadows there is a discarded candy wrapper from the childish desire we just prayed off last night—the lingering evidence of some little temper or temptation that only the Father can see hiding within His supposedly "all grown-up" little child.

It is He alone whom we must trust to see the very worst in us, yet still think the very best of us. It is simply the love of a Father. It is the unfailing love of a Father whose son should have been old enough to receive his inheritance without acting like a child, without wandering off into failure and stumbling down the mine shaft of lasciviousness. Nevertheless, the Father's love throws a party for the prodigal and prepares a feast for the foolish (see Luke 15:11-32). Comprehend with childhood faith the love of the Father we have in God!

POWER

It is God alone whom we must trust to see the very worst in us, yet still think the very best of us.

In Matthew chapter 6, when the disciples asked Jesus to teach them to pray, the first thing He taught them was to acknowledge the *fatherhood* of God. When we say "Our Father," we acknowledge His fatherhood and declare our relationship with Him as it relates to the privilege of belonging to His divine family. Similarly, one of the first words most babies say is "Daddy." So knowing your father helps you understand your own identity as a son or daughter. Greater still is the need to know not only *who* my father is, but *how he feels about me.*

It is not good to deny a child the right to feel his father's love. In divorce cases, some women use the children to punish their ex-husbands. Because of her broken covenant with the child's father, the mother may deny him the right to see his child. This is not good for the child! Every child is curious about his father.

> *Philip saith unto Him, Lord, show us the Father, and it sufficeth us* (John 14:8).

Philip didn't know who the Father was, but he longed to see Him. I can still remember what it was like to fall asleep watching television and have my father pick up my listless, sleep-ridden frame from the couch and carry me up the stairs to bed. I would wake up to the faint smell of his Old Spice cologne and feel his strong arms around me, carrying me as if I weighed nothing at all. I never felt as safe and protected as I did in the arms of my father—that is, until he died and I was forced to seek refuge in the arms of my heavenly Father.

What a relief to learn that God can carry the load even better than my natural father could, and that He will never leave me nor forsake me! Perhaps it was this holy refuge that inspired the hymnist to pen the hymn, "What a fellowship, what a joy divine. Leaning on the everlasting arms."[1]

Fear and Pain

I have been in the delivery room with my wife as she was giving birth. I witnessed the pain and suffering she endured. I believe that there were times of such intense pain that she would have shot me if she had had a chance. Her desire made her continue. She didn't simply give up. She endured the pain so new life could be born. Once the child was born, the pain was soon forgotten.

Until the desire to go forward becomes greater than the memories of past pain, you will never hold the power to create again. However, when the desire comes back into your spirit and begins to live in you again, it will release you from the pain.

Some years ago I was birthing my ministry in terms of evangelism. I was preaching in places most up-and-coming ministers would not want to go. It was not at all uncommon for me to drive for hours into some rural, secluded "back-woods" area to minister to a handful of people who were often financially, and in some cases mentally, deprived! God teaches men character in the most deplorable of classrooms. So He had me in school. I thought I was traveling to minister to the people, but in actuality God was taking me through a series of hurdles and obstacles in order to strengthen my legs for the sprints ahead.

It was while on one of these pilgrimages into the unknown that I ministered in an area and then returned to the little place I was staying. The room I was given had a bed so bowed it looked like a musical instrument. The entire house was infested with flies. I have never before or after seen so many flies attracted to a house. I have often mused over the great possibility of satanic activity and witchcraft in that house. I can remember being horrified at the filth and slime that existed in the bathroom, and lying in my bed at night praying for the grace not to run.

POWER

Until the desire to go forward becomes greater than the memories of past pain, you will never hold the power to create again.

LIVING

While attempting to act as though I were comfortable in this inhumane environment, I encountered some children who came over to talk to me. I noticed immediately that most of them were either physically or mentally abnormal. These abnormalities ranged in severity from slurred speech to missing fingers and dwarfed limbs. Nevertheless, they were playing and laughing as children do who have been given the mercy of blindness to the wretchedness of their circumstances. One little boy came over and whispered in my ear. He said, "That little boy turning somersaults is my cousin-brother." It seemed that the little boy was the product of some hot summer night when need had overruled common sense and the little boy's mother had slept with her own brother and produced a mutated offspring that halted around as a testimony to their impropriety.

Suddenly I began to understand that these children were the result of inordinate affections and incestuous relationships! These are the twisted hands and stumped feet of children forever incapacitated by the sins of their parents. This plight is unnecessary; it could have been avoided. So are the children of the mind: the crippled need we sometimes have to receive the accolades of men; the twisted, angry tears that flood cold pillows in the night because we are left holding the offspring of yesterday's mistakes in our arms. Like a young girl left saddled with a child she can hardly rear, we wonder what we could have been if one thing or another had not happened.

There is a difference, however, between these natural children and the crippled ones that haunt the recesses of our minds. There is a difference between psychological and biological offspring. To abort a biological child is wrong. To abort psychological offspring is deliverance. I am not talking about aborting biological babies—I am talking about aborting every psychological baby that is growing in the womb of our minds. Every remaining embryo that ties us to a dead issue can be and must be aborted!

You don't have to leave some grossly deformed generation of problems that beget more problems! God has given you power over the enemy! This power is not rejoicing power, to sing or preach. It's not power over people and external dilemmas. He has given you the power to abort the seeds of failure. Abortion is a strong term, but effective in this case. Pull down the strongholds. Pull down those things that have taken a strong hold on your life. If you don't pull them down, they will refuse to relinquish their grip. It will take an act of your will and God's power to stop the spiritual unborn from manifesting in your life. God will not do it without you—but He will do it through you.

> *(For the weapons of our warfare are not carnal, but mighty through God to the pulling down of strong holds;) casting down imaginations, and every high thing that exalteth itself against the knowledge of God, and bringing into captivity every thought to the obedience of Christ* (2 Corinthians 10:4-5).

These thoughts, wounds, and emotional oddities are self-exalting. They establish themselves as god in your life. They endeavor to control or manipulate you. These progeny of lesser days want to crown themselves as indications of your destiny. How can you afford to submit your future to the discretion of your past? The greatest freedom you have is the freedom to change your mind. Enthroned in the recesses of your mind may be some antichrist that would desire to keep you connected to what you have forsaken. Cast it down! The Bible says to repent. Repentance is when the mind decides to organize a mutiny and overthrow the government that controlled it in the past. As long as these other things reign in your life, Christ's seat is taken because these thoughts and feelings of the past are sitting on the throne. If they are on the throne, then Christ is on the Cross. Put Christ on the throne and your past on the Cross.

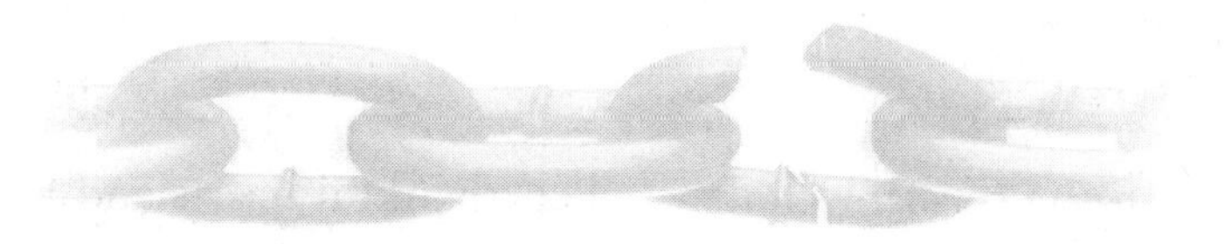

First, let me rebuke the spirit of fear. Fear will hide in the closet as we are blessed and make strange noises when no one else is around. We need to declare God to this fear. We dare not fall in love with what God is doing, but we must always be in love with who God is. God does not change. That's why we must set our affections on things that are eternal. He said, *"For I am the Lord, I change not"* (Mal. 3:6a). It is such a comfort, when the chilly voice of fear speaks, to know that God doesn't change.

> His purpose doesn't change. His methods may change, but His ultimate purpose doesn't. People have a need to know what comes next. God doesn't always make us privy to such information, but He has promised that if we walk uprightly, He will not withhold any good thing from us (see Ps. 84:11). I therefore conclude that if God withheld it, then it was no longer working for my good. I am then ready for the next assignment—it will be good for me.

In the special moments when thankful hearts and hands lifted in praise come into corporate levels of expression with memories of what could have happened had God not intervened, we find our real ministry. Above all titles and professions, every Christian is called to be a worshiper. We are a royal priesthood that might have become extinct had the mercy of the Lord not arrested the villainous horrors of the enemy. Calloused hands are raised in praise—hands that tell a story of struggle, whether spiritual or natural. These holy hands that we raise unto the Lord are the hands of people who, like Jonah, have lived through a personal hell. Who could better thank the Lord than the oppressed who were delivered by the might of a loving God whose love is tempered with the necessary ability to provoke change?

God wants to give us the strength to overcome past pain and move forward into new life. Solomon wrote, "*Where there is no vision, the people perish*" (Prov. 29:18a). Vision is the desire to go ahead. Until you have a vision to go ahead, you will always live in yesterday's struggles. God is calling you to today. The devil wants you to live in yesterday. He's always telling you about what you cannot do. His method is to bring up your past. He wants to draw your attention backward.

Expect something wonderful to happen!

God wants to put desire in the spirit of broken women and men. There wouldn't be any desire if there wasn't any relationship. You can't desire something that's not there. The very fact that you have a desire is in itself an indication that better days are coming. David said, "*I had fainted, unless I had believed to see the goodness of the Lord in the land of the living*" (Ps. 27:13). Expect something wonderful to happen.

When I was a boy, we had a dog named Pup. Don't let the name fool you, though. He was a mean and ferocious animal.

He would eat anyone who came near him. We had him chained in the back of the house to a four-by-four post. The chain was huge. We never imagined that he could possibly tear himself loose from that post. When he chased something, the chain would snap him back. We often laughed at him, as we stood outside his reach.

One day Pup saw something that he really wanted. It was out of his reach. However, the motivation before him became more important than what was behind him. He pulled that chain to the limit. All at once, instead of drawing him back, the chain snapped, and Pup was loose to chase his prey.

That's what God will do for you. The thing that used to pull you back will snap, and you will be liberated by a goal because God has put greatness before you. You can't receive what God wants for your life by looking back. He is mighty. He is powerful enough to destroy the yoke of the enemy in your life. He is strong enough to bring you out and loose you, deliver you, and set you free.

POWER POINTS FOR LIVING

1. God still speaks to the childhood issues of the aging heart. This is the ministry that only a Father can give. What childhood issues would you like your heavenly Father to heal for you? Believe He will heal them.

2. God knows your innermost needs. List a few and believe that He will meet them.

3. It is Him alone whom we must trust to see the very worst in us, yet still think the very best of us. Name a "worst" thing about you—and a "best" thing. Believe God only sees the best!

4. God will never leave you nor forsake you! Name a few people who have let you down. Have you forgiven them? Believe that God will never let you down.

5. Until the desire to go forward becomes greater than the memories of past pain, you will never hold the power to create again. Can you trust God enough to forge ahead? Believe that He will open the right doors for you to walk through to a glorious future.

6. Expect something wonderful to happen. Write something wonderful that you would like to have happen. Do you believe it is God's will for this to happen? Believe it will.

7. God's powerful anointing will loose you, deliver you, and set you free from fear. What is your greatest fear? Believe that you *can and will overcome that fear* through the power of God's mercy and grace.

ENDNOTE

1. Elisha A. Hoffman and Anthony J. Showalter, "Leaning on the Everlasting Arms," 1887.

CHAPTER 8

POWER TO BELIEVE

What we need is a seed in the womb that we believe is enough to produce an embryo. We must be willing to feed that embryo for it to grow and become visible. When it will not be hidden anymore, it will break forth in life as answered prayer. It will break forth. No matter how hard others try to hold it back, it will break forth.

Put the truth in your spirit, and feed, nurture, and allow it to grow. Quit telling yourself you're "too fat, too old, too late, or too ignorant." Quit feeding yourself that garbage. That will not nourish the baby. Too often we starve the embryo of faith that is growing within us. It is unwise to speak against your own body. Speak life to your body. Celebrate who you are. You are the image of God.

Scriptures remind us of who we are. "*I will praise Thee; for I am fearfully and wonderfully made: marvellous are Thy works; and that my soul knoweth right well*" (Ps. 139:14). These are the words that will feed our souls. The truth will allow new life to swell up within us. Feed the embryo within with words such as these:

> *When I consider Thy heavens, the work of Thy fingers, the moon and the stars, which Thou hast ordained; what is man, that Thou*

> *art mindful of him? and the son of man, that Thou visitest him?* (Psalms 8:3-4)
>
> *And the Lord shall make thee the head, and not the tail; and thou shalt be above only, and thou shalt not be beneath...* (Deuteronomy 28:13).
>
> *I can do all things through Christ which strengtheneth me* (Philippians 4:13).

The Word of God will provide the nourishment that will feed the baby inside.

POWER

The Word of God provides nourishment.

LIVING

The Book of Hebrews provides us with a tremendous lesson on faith. When we believe God, we are counted as righteous. Righteousness cannot be earned or merited. It comes only through faith. We can have a good report simply on the basis of our faith. Faith becomes the tender, like money is the legal tender in this world that we use for exchange of goods and services. Faith becomes the tender, or the substance, of things hoped for, and the evidence of things not seen. By it the elders obtained a good report (see Heb. 11:1-2).

> *Through faith we understand that the worlds were framed by the word of God, so that things which are seen were not made of things which do appear* (Hebrews 11:3).

The invisible became visible and was manifested. God wants us to understand that just because we can't see it, doesn't mean that He won't do it. What God wants to do in us begins as a word that gets in the spirit. Everything that is tangible started as an intangible. It was a dream, a thought, a word of God. In the same way, what humankind has invented began as a concept in someone's mind. So just because we don't see it, doesn't mean we won't get it.

POWER

God wants us to understand that just because we can't see it, doesn't mean that He won't do it.

There is a progression in the characters mentioned in this chapter of Hebrews. Abel worshiped God by faith. Enoch walked with God by faith. You can't walk with God until you worship God. The first calling is to learn how to worship God. When you learn how to worship God, then you can develop a walk with Him. Stop trying to get people to walk with God who won't worship. If you don't love Him enough to worship, you'll never be able to walk with Him. If you can worship like Abel, then you can walk like Enoch.

POWER

When you learn how to worship God, then you can develop a walk with Him.

LIVING

Enoch walked, and by faith Noah worked with God. You can't work with God until you walk with God. You can't walk with God until you worship God. If you can worship like Abel, then you can walk like Enoch. And if you walk like Enoch, then you can work like Noah.

> *But without faith it is impossible to please Him: for he that cometh to God must believe*

that He is, and that He is a rewarder of them that diligently seek Him (Hebrews 11:6).

God will reward those who persevere in seeking Him. He may not come when you want Him to, but He will be right on time. If you will wait on the Lord, He will strengthen your heart. He will heal you and deliver you. He will lift you up and break those chains. God's power will loose the bands from around your neck. He will give you the garment of praise for the spirit of heaviness (see Isa. 61:3).

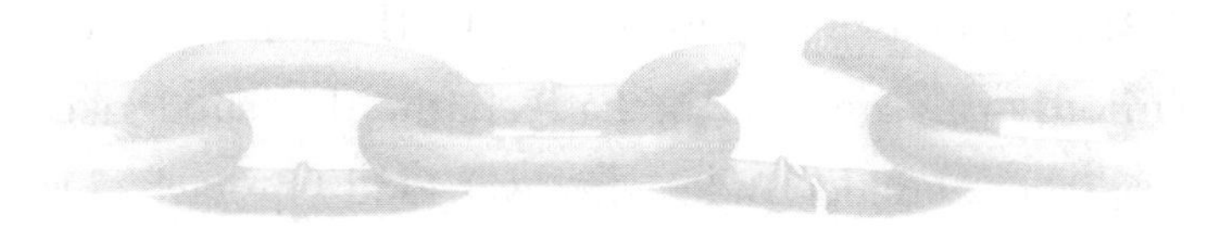

The letter to the Philadelphia church, the church of brotherly love, basically ends with the words, "I am the One who closes doors." (See Revelation 3.) The art to surviving painful moments is living in the "yes" zone. We need to learn to respond to God with a yes when the doors are open, and a yes when they are closed. Our prayer must be:

I trust Your decisions, Lord; and I know that if this relationship is good for me, You will allow it to continue. I know that if the door is closed, then it is also for my good. So I say "yes" to You as I go into this relationship. I appreciate brotherly love, and I still say "yes" if You close the door.

This is the epitome of a trust that is seldom achieved, but is to be greatly sought after. In so doing, you will be able to savor the gift of companionship without the fear of reprisal!

Abraham was a great man of faith. The writer of Hebrews mentions many areas of Abraham's faith. Abraham looked for a city whose builder and maker was God (see Heb. 11:10). However, he is not listed in the faith "hall of fame" as the one who produced Isaac. If Abraham was famous for anything, it should have been for producing Isaac. However, he is not applauded for that.

"Through faith also Sara herself received strength to conceive seed, and was delivered of a child when she was past age, because she judged Him faithful who had promised" (Heb. 11:11). When it comes to bringing forth the baby, the Scriptures do not refer to a man; they refer to a womb-man.

Sarah needed power to conceive seed when she was past childbearing age. God met her need. She believed that He was capable of giving her a child regardless of what the circumstances looked like. From a natural perspective, it was impossible. The enemy certainly didn't want it to happen. God, however, performed His promise.

Fear or Respect?

> *And unto man He said, Behold, the fear of the Lord, that is wisdom; and to depart from evil is understanding* (Job 28:28).

The Hebrew term for "fear" in this verse is yir'ah, according to *Strong's Exhaustive Concordance of the Bible*. It means a moral fear, or reverence. So what attitude should we have toward our heavenly Father? The Bible declares that we should have a strong degree of reverence for Him. But a distinction must be made here: there is a great deal of difference between fear and reverence.

The term *reverence* means to respect or revere; but the term *fear* carries with it a certain connotation of terror and intimidation. That kind of fear is not a healthy attitude for a child of God to have about his heavenly Father. The term rendered *fear* in Job 28:28 could be better translated as "respect." Fear will drive man away from God like it drove Adam to hide in the bushes at the sound of the voice of his only Deliverer. Adam said, *"I heard Thy voice in the garden, and I was afraid..."* (Gen. 3:10). That is not the reaction a loving father wants from his children. I don't want my children to scatter and hide like mice when I approach! I may not always agree with what they have done, but I will always love who they are.

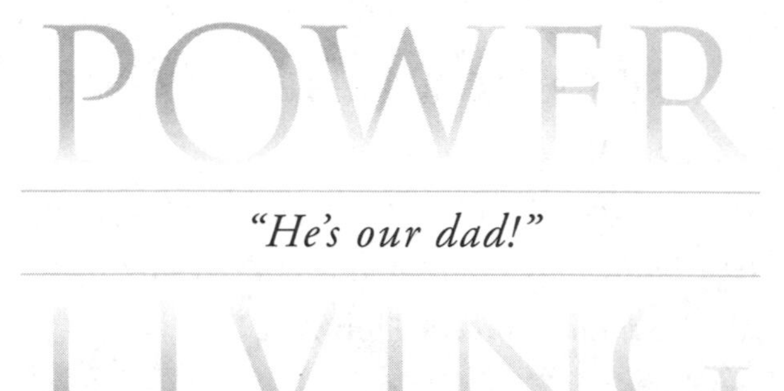

"He's our dad!"

I remember an occasion when some students from the elementary school my sons attended saw me for the first time. Because I stand a good 6' 2" tall, and weigh 250-plus pounds, the little children were completely astonished. The other children told my sons, "Look at how big your dad is! I bet he would just about kill you. Aren't you afraid of him?" My sons quickly responded with glee, "Afraid of him? Nah, he's not mean. He's our dad!" They were not afraid of my stature because they were secure in our relationship. Does that mean they have never been punished? Of course not! What it does mean is they have never been abused! My love holds my judgment in balance.

As imperfect as I admit I am, if I know how to love my children, what about God? Oh friend, He may not approve of your conduct, but He still loves you! In fact, when you come to understand this fact, it will help you improve your conduct.

> *Or despisest thou the riches of His goodness and forbearance and longsuffering; not knowing that the goodness of God leadeth thee to repentance?* (Romans 2:4)

If this text is true (and it is), then we must tell of God's goodness to those who need to repent. I believe *the Church has confused conviction with condemnation.* The Holy Spirit convicts us of sin. *Conviction* leads us to a place of deliverance and change. *Condemnation* leads us to the gallows of despair and hopelessness.

Why have we withheld from so many bleeding hearts the good news of the Gospel? We have replaced this good news with the rambunctious ramblings of self-righteous rhetoric! I believe that we must assume the ministry of reconciliation and cause all people to be reconciled back to their God. There is no healing for the sins of man in the bushes of this world. Regardless of the atrocious behavior we discover when we work with the flawed material of human insufficiency, we must remember that the only antidote is in the presence of the Lord. I am convinced that the very people who need healing the most have been driven away from the only Healer they will ever find in this world.

Nowhere to Hide

There is no tiptoeing around the presence of God with

pristine daintiness—as if we could tiptoe softly enough not to awaken a God who never sleeps nor slumbers. We shuffle in His presence like children who were instructed not to disturb their father, although God isn't sleepy and He doesn't have to go to work. He is alive and awake, and He is well. We blare like trumpets announcing our successes, but we whisper our failures through parched lips in the shadows of our relationship with Him. We dare not air our inconsistencies with arrogance because we know we are so underdeveloped and dependent upon Him for everything we need.

POWER

When a person hides himself from God, he loses himself.

LIVING

It is the nature of a fallen humanity to hide from God. Adam hid from God. How ridiculous it is for us to think that we can hide from Him! His intelligence supersedes our frail ability to be deceptive. Adam hid himself. No wonder we are lost. We have hidden ourselves. We didn't hide our work or our gifts; we have hidden ourselves.

When a person hides himself from God, he loses himself. What good is it to know where everything else is, if we cannot find ourselves? Our loss causes a desperation that produces sin and separation. Like the prodigal son in chapter 15 of Luke's Gospel, in our desperation we need to come to ourselves and come out from under the bushes where we have hidden ourselves. We need to become transparent in the presence of the Lord.

Adam's meager attempt at morality caused him to sew together a few leaves in a figgy little apron that was dying even while he was sewing it. Why would a lost man cover himself with leaves? Adam said, "I was afraid." Fear separated this son from his Father; fear caused him to conspire to deceive his only Solution. This fear was not reverence—it was desperation.

POWER

If Adam had only run toward instead of away from God, he could have been delivered!

If Adam had only run *toward* instead of *away* from God, he could have been delivered! Why then do we continue to present a God who cannot be approached to a dying world? Many in the Christian family are still uncomfortable with their heavenly Father. Some Christians do not feel accepted in the Beloved. They feel that their relationship with God is meritorious, but they are intimidated because of His holiness. I admit that His holiness all the more exposes our flawed, soiled personhood. Yet His grace allows us to approach Him—though we are not worthy—through the bloody skins soaked with Christ's blood.

We are properly draped and dressed to come into the presence of a Holy God only because His accepted Son, Jesus Christ, has wrapped us in His own identity. Like Adam, we are draped by a bloody sacrifice that has made it possible for us to approach our Father and live.

> *Neither is there any creature that is not manifest in His sight: but all things are naked and opened unto the eyes of Him with whom we have to do* (Hebrews 4:13).

It is futile to hide from our Father. It is His intelligence (often referred to as His omniscience) that exposes us! We cannot alter His ability to see, so we need to develop enough security to be comfortable with His intelligence. Who else knows you like God does? If you hide from His perfect love, you will never be able to enjoy a relationship with your heavenly Father and be comfortable enough to sit in His lap.

Peter said, "*...To whom shall we go?*" (John 6:68). The truth is that we have no one else to turn to; yet for some reason, we don't seem to know how to come to Him. We don't realize that we can be accepted by Him and find tender mercy and healing for the scars of life and for our bruised hearts—until our desperation, fear, and separation cause us to seek shelter in the presence of the Lord.

IT TAKES TRUST

> *He that dwelleth in the secret place of the most High shall abide under the shadow of the Almighty. I will say of the Lord, He is my refuge and my fortress: my God: in Him will I trust* (Psalms 91:1-2).

POWER

The basis of any relationship must be trust.

The basis of any relationship must be trust. Trusting God with your successes isn't really a challenge. The real test of trust is to be able to share your secrets, your inner failures and fears. A mutual enhancement comes into a relationship where there is intimacy based on honesty.

Jesus told the woman at the well, a woman whose flaws and failures He had supernaturally revealed, "*...true worshippers shall worship the Father in spirit and in truth: for the Father seeketh such [real people, flawed people like the woman at the well] to worship Him. God is a Spirit: and they that worship Him must worship Him in spirit and in truth*" (John 4:23-24).

POWER

God knows our thoughts even as we unconsciously gather them together to make sense in our own minds!

LIVING

We have nothing to fear, for our honesty with the Father doesn't reveal anything to Him that He doesn't already know! His intellect is so keen that He doesn't have to wait for you to make a mistake. He knows of your failure before you fail. His knowledge is all-inclusive, spanning the gaps between times and incidents. He knows our thoughts even as we unconsciously gather them together to make sense in our own minds!

> *The Lord knoweth the thoughts of man, that they are vanity* (Psalms 94:11).

Once we know this, all our attempts at silence and secrecy seem juvenile and ridiculous. He is "the all-seeing One," and He knows perfectly and completely what is in each of us. When we pray, and more importantly, when we commune with God, we must have the kind of confidence and assurance that neither requires nor allows deceit.

Although my Father abhors my sin, He loves me. His love is incomprehensible, primarily because there is nothing with which we can compare it! What we must do is accept the riches of His grace and stand in the shade of His loving arms.

POWER

We need to lay before Him and seek His face in the beauty of holiness.

LIVING

We need to lay ourselves before Him and seek His face in the beauty of holiness—the holiness that produces wholeness. This isn't a matter of one denomination arguing with another over who is right; it is a matter of a broken family seeking healing and answers that can only come from the presence of God.

The Old Testament expressed the righteousness of God, a righteousness that the New Testament fully revealed in the

Gospel of Jesus Christ. Although the Old Testament could not completely reveal the righteousness of God, it certainly introduced a concept of how God defines holiness to humanity and Israel.

God knew that the children of Israel would fail in their attempts to achieve the morality contained in the Law. Through their failures, God wanted the Israelites to find the redemption that He had allocated through the blood. Unfortunately, instead of honestly confessing to God the enormity of their failure, they became increasingly hypocritical. The whole purpose of the Law was spoiled because the fleshly egos of men would not repent and seek divine assistance for justification.

> *For I am not ashamed of the gospel of Christ: for it is the power of God unto salvation to every one that believeth; to the Jew first, and also to the Greek. For therein is the righteousness of God revealed from faith to faith: as it is written, The just shall live by faith* (Romans 1:16-17).

Writing in all honesty, the greatest of the apostles—the writer of most of the New Testament epistles—confessed that though he aspired to "apprehend," he hadn't attained (see Phil. 3:12). In what area did this apostle fail? The Holy Spirit has granted him some semblance of diplomatic immunity that at least affords him the right of privacy in spite of imperfections. Yet we continually eat a perfect word from his stained hands, a word that converts the soul and challenges the most godly among us. I speak, of course, of the apostle Paul.

> *Brethren, I count not myself to have apprehended: but this one thing I do, forgetting those things which are behind, and reaching forth unto those things which are before, I press toward the mark for the prize of the high calling of God in Christ Jesus* (Philippians 3:13-14).

Alas, the call is a high calling. Yet it has been answered by lowly people who had the discernment to see a God high and lifted up. They stood on their toes like children, but still fell short of reaching His splendor. In short, the heroes in the Bible were not perfect, but they were powerful! They were not superhuman, but they were revelatory. Often chastised and corrected, they were still not discarded, for the Lord was with them.

POWER POINTS FOR LIVING

1. Celebrate who you are. You are the image of God. What does "the image of God" mean to you?

2. You can't walk with God until you worship Him. What is your favorite way to worship God?

3. Conviction leads to deliverance and change. Have you been convicted lately? How did you handle it?

4. If Adam had only run *toward* instead of *away* from God, he could have been delivered! Write about a time when you ran away from God instead of toward Him.

5. We must accept the riches of His grace, and stand in the shade of His loving arms. Why is it so hard sometimes to accept God's gifts?

6. We need to lay ourselves before Him and seek His face in the beauty of holiness—the holiness that produces wholeness. Describe "the beauty of holiness."

7. Through our failures, God wants us to find the redemption that He has allocated through the blood of Jesus. Do you believe that the blood of Jesus covers *all* your sins and failures? Thank Him in a prayer.

CHAPTER 9

ANOINTED POWER

Why do the heathen rage, and the people imagine a vain thing? The kings of the earth set themselves, and the rulers take counsel together, against the Lord, and against His anointed, saying, let us break their bands asunder, and cast away their cords from us. He that sitteth in the heavens shall laugh: the Lord shall have them in derision. Then shall He speak unto them in His wrath, and vex them in His sore displeasure. Yet have I set my king upon my holy hill of Zion. I will declare the decree: the Lord hath said unto Me, Thou art my Son; this day have I begotten Thee. Ask of Me, and I shall give Thee the heathen for Thine inheritance, and the uttermost parts of the earth for Thy possession (Psalms 2:1-8).

Why do the heathen rage and the people imagine a vain thing? The actual question in this text is not King David asking God the motivation of those who take counsel (conspire) to come against the Lord and His anointed. More importantly, it is David asking God why He allows it to happen. "God, why do You allow the heathen to rage, and why do You let the rulers and kings of the earth set themselves against You and against Your anointed? Why God, why?"

The Question Is Why

Why does God allow His anointed to suffer so greatly? After all, the sole motivation of the anointed is to do the will of God. You would think that if the primary desire in the life of the anointed is to please their heavenly Father, the least He could do is protect and preserve them. You would think God would stop the persecution, mistreatment, and abuse by the heathens and phony church folks. But the truth of the matter is that God allows, and in most cases sends, His anointed through more than all others. An intelligent question is, "God, why?'

An intelligent question is, "God, why?"

The anointed might say, "Why do You let this mess happen when I'm obeying You? Why do You let people treat me like this? God, what's up with that? Are You a sadist who enjoys inflicting pain on others? Oh God, why allow these heathens to trip on me like this? I mean, after all, I'm a man of God, I'm a woman of God. I don't have to take this kind of treatment from some stupid unsaved employer who doesn't even respect the fact that I'm called, appointed, and anointed. Hey, these people don't even know You. I do!

"Therefore, I should be afforded special privileges. I should not have to wait until I mature and develop character to get whatsoever I desire—I'm a King's kid! I should be able to just name it and claim it. I have the keys to the Kingdom. I can call what I want into existence. I thought all I had to do is say the Word, right?"

But you know what God's response is to all that selfishness and flesh? *"No...I...don't...think...so!"*

Let us look at the psalmist's question in this passage and address each point, one by one.

"WHYS" OF THE ANOINTED

> *The kings of the earth set themselves, and the rulers take counsel together* [conspiring together], *against the Lord, and against His anointed* (Psalms 2:2).

"Against the Lord." The most prevailing sin of all humankind is the sin of selfishness...the idolizing of self (self-idolatry). Selfishness is the epitome of satanic, demonic, and rebellious sinful motivations and behavior. Observing the power and majesty of Almighty God, satan became

jealous of the Lord's glory. Satan sought to instigate a mutiny in Heaven.

Jealousy is the manifestation of insecurity and dissatisfaction with one's calling and self-worth. When you don't know your purpose, you become discontented and often envious of another's success. Jealousy and bitter envying are the root cause of the spirit of competition. That spirit presently plagues many in church leadership and those aspiring to positions of leadership. Everybody wants to be number one, the top dog, the head honcho, the man or woman in demand.

So in our desire to be number one, we covet, lust, and compete for another's position, status, or possessions. Why do we do this? Because we want everybody to look at us, to like us, to admire us, to respect us, to worship us. Before we know it, we've become drunk with selfish ambition and, like satan, our hidden motives of the heart become the attitude of rebellion against who and what God has called us to be and do. If we don't come to our senses and repent, we will inevitably become deceived and overwhelmed with the lust for power, prestige, position, and possessions. We no longer aspire to love the Lord with all our heart, soul, strength, and mind.

The confessions and attitudes of our hearts reflect the central sentiment of satan: "I will exalt myself above the throne of God, above the throne of my husband, above the throne of my employer or supervisor. *My* church will be bigger than the Baptist church down the street. I'm going to be more popular and bigger than the other TV evangelist. I will; I...I...I...I will exalt myself."

Because you were not patient enough to wait on God's timing (even though you've been called, you need to wait until you are sent), you've aligned yourself with the wicked rulers of the day and taken counsel against the Lord. Why? Selfishness!

POWER

If we don't repent, we will become deceived with the lust for power, prestige, position, and possessions.

LIVING

"And against His anointed." It is without exception, absolutely necessary for the anointed to suffer. The moment you begin to accept and understand this, you will begin to rejoice in tribulation. I know this doesn't sit well with much of what we've been taught in reference to our victory in Christ. We do have victory in Christ, but we must understand that there has to be a battle fought in order to gain a victory. There is no victory without war. Also you have to know that just as God has promised to supply all our needs according to His riches in glory, He also has promised us

trials and tribulations in this life. Tribulations and trials serve, by the aid of the Holy Spirit, a divine purpose. The purpose is death. Death? That's right, I mean death—death to the flesh.

POWER

There is no victory without war.

LIVING

If you are going to walk in the anointing, power, and presence of God, you must be dead to self. In order to be alive to Christ, you must first yield to the sanctifying work of the Holy Spirit and die to the works of the flesh. Why? *So that no flesh may glory in His sight.* Before a man or woman is dead to self, they are occupied and consumed with self and how they can please themselves. They make a conscious decision to walk in their own understanding, instead of acknowledging the Lord and being directed by His wisdom.

Submission + Suffering + Obedience + Praise = Anointing (Power for Living)

And Samuel said, Hath the Lord as great delight in burnt offerings and sacrifices, as in

> *obeying the voice of the Lord? Behold, to obey is better than sacrifice, and to hearken than the fat of rams. For rebellion is as the sin of witchcraft, and stubbornness is as iniquity and idolatry. Because thou hast rejected the word of the Lord, He has also rejected thee from being king* (1 Samuel 15:22-23).

Like King Saul, selfish Christians are charismatic witches. They rebel against totally submitting to the Lordship of Christ Jesus (the Anointed). Like King Saul, selfish, carnal Christians and Christian leaders are idolaters of self. They stubbornly insist upon doing things their way instead of God's way. Selfish people (self-idolaters) sometimes are a god unto themselves. Just like King Saul and Samson the judge, they will awake one day to find that the glory (the anointing) has departed (that is, if they were ever anointed in the first place).

Anointed people are in great demand by those who need the touch of God in their lives. Because anointed people have the ability to draw from the resources of God's miracle-working power in time of desperate need, people have a tendency to worship and make idols out of them. But God says He shares His glory with no one. God is a jealous God (see Exod. 20:5). God will not bestow His Holy Spirit upon some flaky, selfish Christian who is engrossed with selfish ambition, trying to build a kingdom at the expense of using

God's anointing. Many ministries try to build their own personal kingdoms, while rationalizing that they are building God's Church. The devil is a liar and the truth is not in him (see John 8:44).

Why are the anointed persecuted? Anointed people are free people. The Word of God says that *"where the Spirit of the Lord is, there is liberty"* (2 Cor. 3:17). Wicked leadership and stubborn, sedate people who have taken counsel against the Lord, do not like free people, because free people can't be controlled.

Anointed people are full of the Holy Ghost. Life in the Holy Ghost is righteousness, peace, and joy. Anointed people are people who have been burdened by the Cross of Calvary and are no longer bound by the sins and embarrassments of old lifestyles.

Anointed men and women of God know that because of the precious blood shed by Jesus Christ they have right-standing with the Father—they possess power for living. When they think about the goodness of Jesus, and all that He's done for them, their very souls cry out, "Hallelujah!" They begin to praise God with unrestrained zeal and passion. That, my brothers and sisters, is what gives you joy unspeakable and full of glory, the anointed presence of the Holy Spirit.

Controlling people (like those rulers who wanted to keep the people from praising Jesus) find that type of ecstatic praise to be very irritating and irrational. They want you to be composed and dignified at all times. Why? Because instead of giving praise and worship to Jesus, they unknowingly (and some knowingly) want you to praise them—the great "Doctor So-and-So" and the wonderful "Mother Who-dun-it." But again, the devil is a liar!

POWER

Anointed people are full of the Holy Ghost.

LIVING

The heathen declare *"Let us break their bands asunder, and cast away their cords from us"* (Ps. 2:3). The word *bands* means "chains and cords or fetters attached around the feet to restrict movement." The psalmist signifies unity in the illustration. The anointed people of God often find themselves in conflict with those who have personal agendas that are contrary to the will of God. Persecution is a mandatory by-product of being anointed of God. You would think that since your motivations and intentions are only to do God's will and minister to God's people, everybody, especially Christian folks, would love you and appreciate you so much. Not so. Therefore, the all-encompassing question comes to mind, Why not?

The anointing of God has the innate and wonderful ability to soften hard hearts, break stiff necks, crush pride, and tear down the walls of strife and division. This inevitably will bring sincere men and women to repentance. A repented heart is soft and gentle. Gentle hearts are receptive to reconciliation. Reconciliation is the hallmark of love. Love and forgiveness are the cornerstone and foundation that build.

POWER

The anointing of God has power to soften hard hearts, break stiff necks, crush pride, and tear down walls of strife and division.

LIVING

So why do the heathen seek to divide the people of God? Simply put, so there will not be any anointing. Nothing can wither up and dry out the fresh spring well of the Spirit's anointing faster than strife, division (two different visions), and discord. The Bible says, "Six things does the Lord hate and the seventh is an abomination," the seventh thing being those who sow discord among the brethren (the saints of God). (See Proverbs 6:16-19.) But when we get in accord, seeking the will of God, He will always, without exception, manifest Himself.

> *And when the day of Pentecost was fully come, they were all with one accord in one place. And suddenly there came a sound from heaven as of a rushing mighty wind, and it filled all the house where they were sitting. And there appeared unto them cloven tongues like as of fire, and it sat upon each of them. And they were all filled with the Holy Ghost, and began to speak with other tongues, as the Spirit gave them utterance* (Acts 2:1-4).

Unity evolves around truth-seeking believers who are committed to knowing the heart of Christ. Unity brings about the Spirit's power and anointing.

He Who Sits in the Heavens Laughs

God is pleased and insistent upon being glorified and receiving glory from His creation. Many children of God have become overwhelmed with bewilderment and are confused as to why bad things always seem to happen to good people. But the answer is simple, my friend. God wants to be glorified. So every now and then you may find yourself tempted and pursued like a fugitive, wanted by the devil. The pressure, stress, and strain in your life may make you feel like a hunk of cheese on a mouse trap, ready to be eaten by the enemy. You may get the idea that God is using you like a pawn on the chess board of a game called life—a game over which you have no control and cannot win.

POWER

The pressure, stress, and strain in your life may make you feel like a hunk of cheese on a mouse trap, ready to be eaten by the enemy.

LIVING

The devil gets happy because he thinks you're down for the count. But, God laughs! Why? Because God already knows that He will not allow you to go through anything, or be subjected to anything, beyond your anointing. (See First Corinthians 10:13.) God gives you ability to bear it. That's why He laughs and lets the devil sometimes have at you. God knows you're faithful. God knows that it's just a matter of time before satan pushes you so far that you will fall right back into the lap of goodness and mercy.

Why goodness and mercy? Because goodness and mercy are praise partners. They testify and witness to the goodness of God. They remind us of the fact that no matter how hard the battle, how difficult the trial, we can have assurance that God the Father will never leave us. He will never forsake us. Goodness makes us confident to know that if we will only be still and wait on God, we will eventually and inevitably see the salvation of the Lord. Goodness is God's guarantee that we will get that massive, needed, and overdue "breakthrough."

What about mercy? Sometimes because of being weary from the battle, overwhelmed by the cares of life, or simply because of disobedience or dead works of our flesh, we occasionally give in to temptations. We yield to the lust of the flesh. We might as well be truthful about it. Even though we are not just "sinners saved by grace," we do miss the mark every now and then. In truth, we are the righteousness of God in Christ Jesus and we have right standing with the Father.

However, sometimes we miss it by sinning in our flesh, not our spirit. It is in those times that mercy steps in through the person and blood of Jesus Christ. Mercy pleads our case before the Father. The Bible says we have an advocate with the Father, so that *"if we confess our sins, He is faithful and just to forgive us our sins and to cleanse us from all unrighteousness"* (1 John 1:9). Scripture also says, *"There is therefore now no condemnation to them which are in Christ Jesus, who walk not after the flesh, but after the Spirit"* (Rom. 8:1).

Mercy says, "God, I know he was disobedient; I know he didn't do what You told him to, but can You find it in Your heart to show him just a little mercy? After all, Daddy, he is Your child and You know he really loves You. To the best of his human frailty, he does try to obey You and serve You, so if You would (and I know because of Your goodness You can), will You please forgive him and show him Your mercy? Not just some mercy, or any mercy, but Your mercy."

Mercy steps in through Jesus Christ.

God's mercy is not like any kind of mercy. You cannot possibly compare God's mercy with man's mercy because God's mercy is not based on the condition of what we've done. It is based on what God has done through the shed blood of Jesus Christ. It is through the blood of Jesus Christ that we have redemption of our sins. Our goody-two-shoes behavior doesn't count. So now, we're truly liberated because we no longer have to worry about being good enough. We are accepted and beloved of the Father. Now that's something to shout about!

Man's mercy is a different case. Man's mercy is based

upon your ability to redeem yourself and change your wicked ways. God's mercy and forgiveness are based on His will to redeem you and His ability to empower you with His Spirit to transform you from your wicked ways. Man is inconsistent. God is consistent. Man is wishy-washy. God is stable. Man is flaky and most of the time, helpless. God is wonderful, and all of the time able.

David said, in so many words, "When I sin, please let me fall into His hands and not the hands of man. For man is wicked, cruel and without mercy, but God is loving and forgiving, showing mercy to those who call on His name." (See Second Samuel 24:14.)

God knows that if He can get you in enough trouble with the devil; enough need and lack in your finances; under just the right amount of pressure; experience just so much pain; and go through enough stress and strain, you'll cry out for His help. *"The Lord's hand is not shortened, that it cannot save; neither His ear heavy, that it cannot hear"* (Isa. 59:1). God wants to build in you faithfulness. Your heavenly Father knows that if He can just get you to the end of yourself, you will eventually stop leaning on the arm of your own flesh. You will begin to honestly trust in Him with all your heart, and lean not on your own understanding. But you will in all your ways truly begin to acknowledge Him, not only as Savior, but as Lord (see Prov. 3:5-6).

The Church as a whole must understand it is absolutely imperative that we accept the truth of God's ultimate and universal purpose for all who call on the name of Jesus. We are to be conformed and transformed into the express image of Christ even as Christ was the express image of the Father (see Heb. 1:3). Hebrews says that Jesus was and is the express image of God. That means that Christ represented the perfect and complete person and mind of God the Father.

POWER

If God can get you to the end of yourself, you will eventually stop leaning on the arm of your own flesh.

LIVING

Our ultimate purpose, as citizens of the Kingdom of God and ambassadors of Christ, is to be perfect and complete expressions of the person and power of Jesus Christ. We are to manifest God's will on earth as it is in Heaven. It is way past the hour that we accept this reality. The mandate of the Kingdom is the ministry of reconciliation—reconciling humankind back to God. We must first die to the image of ourselves in order to be transformed into the image of Christ.

This is one of many, if not the primary reason, that God allows us to go through trials and temptations by the enemy. I said He *allows* you to be tempted of the devil; I didn't say He initiates the tempting. If you're not tempted by evil, how do you know you can resist evil? Also, if you're not being tempted by the enemy, it could very well mean that you've submitted to the enemy. Temptation, in and of itself, is not sin. It's surrendering to temptation that is sin.

POWER

Our ultimate purpose is to be perfect and complete expressions of the person and power of Jesus Christ.

LIVING

When we truly represent God, we express His will and manifest His glory. This is why God laughs at the futile attempts of satan to come against and destroy His children. The devil becomes excited when we're at the point of giving up and giving in, ready to throw in the towel. When we're desperate, the devil really believes we will stop trying to live right, stop praying, stop trying to be Christians, and backslide.

BUT GOD LAUGHS

Why? God knows that when we've come to the end of our rope, when we've reached our weakest point and become desperate, it is only then that we totally, unequivocally, without question or complaint, absolutely rely on and trust in Him.

Trust Him when you've prayed every prayer you know how. Trust Him when you've quoted every Scripture you've ever memorized. Trust Him when you've made every faith-filled confession you can muster. Trust Him when you've done all that you know to do and the situation still hasn't changed or there seems to be no healing, salvation, or deliverance in sight. God tells you the same thing He said to the great apostle Paul, "Don't worry, be happy. For when you've done all that you know to do, just stand." "*...My grace is sufficient for thee: for my strength is made perfect in weakness...*" (2 Cor. 12:9).

Therefore, let us, as anointed men and women of God, take the attitude of Paul, "*...Most gladly therefore will I rather glory in my infirmities, that the power of Christ may rest upon me. Therefore I take pleasure in infirmities, in reproaches, in necessities, in persecutions, in distresses for Christ's sake: for when I am weak, then am I strong*" (2 Cor. 12:9-10).

So why do I rejoice in tribulations, trials, and afflictions? Because when I get weak, that's when I get anointed with power for living!

POWER POINTS FOR LIVING

1. If you are going to walk in the anointing and presence of God, you must be dead to self. Are you dead to self? In what areas are you still praying for a breakthrough?

2. The anointing of God has the innate and wonderful ability to soften hard hearts, break stiff necks, crush pride, and tear down the walls of strife and division. Have you witnessed hard hearts being softened? Pride being crushed? In others? In you?

3. God will *not* allow you to go through anything, or be subjected to anything, beyond your anointing. Do you believe this? Give an example.

4. No matter how hard the battle, how difficult the trial, be assured that God

the Father will never leave you. Speak that sentence aloud, then write it, and commit it to your spirit.

5. Mercy steps in through Jesus Christ. Name three people in the Bible who knew the mercy of Jesus firsthand. Do you know His mercy firsthand? Explain.

6. We were created to trust God always, in all ways. Do you trust Him always, in all ways?

7. When you get weak, that's when you get anointed with power for living! Give an example in your life when being weak actually made you strong.

CHAPTER 10

POWER TO PERSIST AND PERSEVERE

Persistence—Holding Fast to Your Confession of Faith

> *Let us draw near with a true heart in full assurance of faith, having our hearts sprinkled from an evil conscience, and our bodies washed with pure water. Let us hold fast the profession of our faith without wavering; (for He is faithful that promised;)* (Hebrews 10:22-23).

My brothers and sisters, you may be going through hell right now. The fact of the matter is you must accept the reality that God the Father, Creator of Heaven and earth, is trying to mold you and transform you. God wants to change you into what He has declared as His purpose for your life, and that which He spoke about in His written Word. That Word says: You are more than a conqueror through Jesus Christ who loves you (see Rom. 8:37). You are the righteousness of God in Christ Jesus (see Rom. 3:22). Greater is He who is in you than he who is in the world (see 1 John 4:4). You have the power to tread upon serpents and scorpions and over all the power of the enemy (see Luke 10:19). No weapon formed against you shall prosper (see Isa. 54:17). You really are the head and not the tail, above and not beneath, the rich and not the poor (see Deut. 28:12-13).

You, my brothers and sisters, are indeed what God's Word says you are. You are to appropriate what the Word says you are and what the Word says you have. It involves more than just "believing and receiving!"

POWER

You are indeed what God's Word says you are!

LIVING

You've got to be able to persist and move forward in the will of God for your life. Your persistence must continue even when everything seems to be falling apart and when it looks like nothing is turning out right. Stop whining. Learn to stand up under pressure. Set the vision of God before you like a flint and move forward full speed ahead with the plan of God. I don't care how many times the lights get cut off. I don't care how many times the water and heat are turned off. I don't care how many times the rent is overdue. I don't care if you don't have a car and have to use the bus to get from point A to point B. I don't care if you have to eat red beans and rice three days a week just to survive. Forget the dumb stuff!

POWER

You have to fight the devil for the vision every step of the way.

LIVING

If God gave you a vision for something, you've got to know the devil will not sit idly by. You have to fight the devil for the vision, tooth and toenail, every single step of the way. It's less intense to take the easy road, the road of trusting in the things and systems of this world. It's always convenient to call Mommy and Daddy, to get a loan, or to compromise your standards and morals for a promotion on the job. It may seem justifiable to embezzle money from the saints of God to make your church or ministry grow. After all, you're just trying to do the work of the Lord, and they owe it to you.

Know, my brothers and sisters, that the world has a particular road to success. The way of the wicked is the path that leads to spiritual, moral, and physical destruction.

The path to true spiritual, moral, physical, and economic success is the road less traveled. It's the straight and narrow road. In order to truly increase, you must first decrease. Before a seed buds and bears fruit, it must first fall into the ground and die. In order to gain your life, you must first lose it for Christ's sake. If you really want to know Christ and the power of His resurrection, you must have fellowship with His sufferings. We've got to stop being enemies of the Cross. We must take up our cross and bear it daily. The going has always been rough, so we might as well set our minds to get tough. Don't just praise God when everything seems fine and well. We've got to start learning how to cry out to Him in praise even when it appears we're going through hell.

God wants to get you to the point that you become as faithful as the patriarch Job. When anointed people get under pressure, like Job they say, "Even though He slay me, yet shall I hope in Him" (see Job 13:15). He wants you to differ from the children of Israel, who only murmured and complained when He brought them out of Egyptian bondage. God knows you're anointed, and anointed people have the qualities of Moses, Paul, Stephen, and Jesus. They are faithful, regardless of the afflictions, unto death. In this, God is greatly glorified.

Downpour of God's Power

After this manner therefore pray ye: Our Father which art in heaven, Hallowed be Thy

> *name. Thy kingdom come. Thy will be done in earth, as it is in heaven. Give us this day our daily bread. And forgive us our debts, as we forgive our debtors. And lead us not into temptation, but deliver us from evil: For Thine is the kingdom, and the power, and the glory, for ever. Amen* (Matthew 6:9-13).

When Jesus taught on prayer, He was teaching us how to steer the ship of life through the boisterous winds of adversity. If we can follow the "manner" of prayer, then we can follow the course of life. In order to pray effectively, we must know the personage of God. Hence He said, "Our Father." This establishes the basis of the relationship that we have with God. He is more than just Creator. He is our Father. We can create something and not be related to it, but if we father it, a part of us will always be in the things we father. So I must know that I am related to God and not just created by Him.

"Which art in heaven" addresses the fact that the God I am related to is the Ruler of the universe. He sits on the circle of the earth. The Bible teaches us that Heaven is God's throne. So when we say, "which art in heaven," we are proclaiming the absolute sovereignty of our Father. We say, in effect, "Not only are You my Father, but You also are uniquely qualified to answer my prayer. You are related to me and empowered to perform." This phrase points directly to God's position.

Now knowing the person and the position of Him, let us praise Him, saying: "I am not ashamed to praise You as I know the extent of Your authority. I take this time to approach You correctly. 'Hallowed be Thy name.' I almost forgot that just because You are my Father, my 'Abba,' that doesn't give me the right to show disrespect for Your position as Ruler in Heaven and earth. So 'hallowed be Thy name' reminds me that I must enter into Your gates with thanksgiving and into Your courts with praise." (See Psalms 100:4.)

Praise will turn God's head. It will get His attention. I dare you to learn how to praise His name. When you praise His name, you are praising His character. He is "above board." He is holy! When praises go up, blessings come down. So here comes the downpour of power. "Thy kingdom come" releases the downpour of the power of God. Praise will cause the very power of God to come down in your life.

But what good is power without purpose? Thus Jesus taught the disciples, "Thy will be done in earth, as it is in heaven." That is a step up from power to purpose. Now the purpose of God comes down to your life. Have you ever gone through a time that God began to show you His purpose in your life? You can't have success without purpose!

"Give us this day our daily bread" deals with the provisions of Heaven coming down. This is more than a prayer; it is a divine direction. After receiving the power in your life, you come to understand the purpose. Never fear; if you know your purpose, God will release the provisions. Then the provisions you couldn't reach at one stage in your life suddenly fall like an early morning drizzle at another stage in your life.

There's nothing like provision to give you the grace to forgive. It is easier to forgive when you discover that your enemies didn't stop the blessing from coming down. Here Jesus teaches His disciples to pray for the penitence of a forgiving heart. "Forgive us our debts, as we forgive our debtors." So penitence also is flowing down from the throne.

Finally, Jesus taught us to seek deliverance from evil. Pray for the problems that still exist at every stage, and better still, at every success in life!

Having briefly examined the progression of the believer through this precious prayer, let us move on to the real point: the turning point. There must come in every person's life a turning point. Without it you can receive all of this power, purpose, provision, and penitence, overcome the problems, but still be burned out. God wants you to receive all of the great successes and accolades that He promised in His Word, but having received them, you must go beyond them to enter a level of understanding. None of this success is as important or as valuable as you initially thought. At this stage of life you begin to reevaluate what you call success.

God gets the glory when He can give you anything and you can turn from all He gave you and still say from your heart, "Lord, I've found nothing as dear to me as You. My greatest treasure is the assurance of Your divine presence in my life. I am giving it all to You. 'For Thine is the kingdom,'—yes, I know I just prayed it down, but here it is. I am giving it back to You. Wait a minute, Lord. I want to say something else. 'And the power.' You can have that too. Oh, and about all that glory I've been getting—it's Yours as well! What? You want to know how long? Forever and ever and ever. It is so! Amen!"

SONSHIP MANIFESTED THROUGH SUFFERING

In Matthew 3:17, the Father says, *"This is my beloved Son, in whom I am well pleased."* I'm not saying that suffering makes one a son. I am a son of God because I have believed on and received the Lord Jesus Christ as my Savior and Lord (see John 1:12). But there is something about suffering that makes your family relationship evident. There is something about suffering that will bring glory to your life. The apostle Paul said he gloried in tribulations.

Apostle Paul gloried in tribulations.

There is something about suffering that builds determination in your life. It is power-filled determination that says, "I don't care how you feel about me, what you think about me, or even who's looking at me. When I feel the need or urge to, I'm going to praise the Lord. You may want me to be quiet, calm, and controlled, but I'm going to bless Him anyway. I've been through too much to let somebody bind or hinder me from giving God praise. The Lord has delivered me and seen me through too many unbearable situations. I've had to shed too many tears of heartache and pain to let somebody stop me from giving God the praise and honor that is due only Him. My situation was so bad that only God could have brought me out."

POWER

God wants to bring you to the point where you will not only be strong when troubles come, but stable.

LIVING

God says, "You're My child and now it's time for show-and-tell. I'm going to resurrect you. I'm going to bring you up out of your downtrodden situation. I'm going to deliver you. I'm going to bring you out. They said you would never be anything, but I'm going to raise you up." God says, "All the chaos, the unresolved issues, and the unexplained situations will begin to make sense. All of it. You had to go through this so you would suffer enough to die." After the dying process, God will say, "I'm going to bring you to a place of resurrection. It's going to be you, but it's not going to be you. You're going to have a new mind and a new attitude. You're going to be able to understand My dealings and workings. You are going to comprehend and clearly grasp My purpose for your life and ministry. You will soon have the vision to see clearly and objectively My will in your life."

God wants to bring you to the point where you will not only be strong when troubles come, but stable. He wants you to stop worrying all the time about the outcome of things. The next time something devastating happens in your life, you need not get upset. You should say, "I have been through this before. I've been lonely before, I've had to cry before, I've suffered before. I have had to press my way through before, and I found out that all things work together for good to them who love the Lord and are called according to His purpose. I'm going to stand here and wait and see how God brings me out. I don't know when the breakthrough will come, or from where it will come, but I do know it's coming. Whom God will use, I may not know."

If we could talk to the three Hebrews who survived the fiery furnace, perhaps they would describe their experience with the Lord in the midst of the fire in this manner:

"When we were nearing the end of the Babylonian sentencing, we knew that this would be the most trying moment of our lives. We were not sure that the Lord would deliver us, but we were sure that He was able. When they snatched us wildly from the presence of the king, the crowd was screaming hysterically, 'Burn them alive! Burn them alive!' Someone said they turned the furnace up seven times hotter than it should have been. We knew it was true for when they opened the door to throw us in, the men who threw us in were burned alive. We landed in the flames in a fright, terrified and trembling. We didn't even notice that the first miracle was our still being there.

"The fire was all over us. Our ropes were ablaze, but our skin seemed undisturbed. We didn't know what was going on. Then something moved over in the smoke and ashes. We were not alone! Out of the smoke came a shining, gleaming.... We never got His name. He never said it. He never said anything. It was His presence that brought comfort in the fire. It was His presence that created protection in the midst of the crisis. Now, we don't mean that the fire went out because He was there. No, it still burned. It was just that the burning wasn't worthy to be compared to the brilliancy of His presence. We never saw Him again. He only showed up when we needed Him most. But one thing was sure: We were glad they drug us from the presence of the wicked one into the presence of the Righteous One! In His presence we learned that, 'No weapon that is formed against thee shall prosper!'" (See Daniel 3 and Isaiah 54:17.)

> *Thou wilt shew me the path of life: in Thy presence is fulness of joy; at Thy right hand there are pleasures for evermore* (Psalms 16:11).

"Where the check will come from, I may not know. Through whom God will give me favor, I may not be certain. There is one thing I can be assured of and that is this—if I can just wait on the Lord, He's going to bring me out victoriously. If He has to move a mountain, do a miracle, or create a wonder, I have faith and confidence that my God will do it. If I just continue to persist, to be steadfast, immovable and always abounding in the work and will of the Lord, I am coming out...and I'll come out shining. He will, to His glory and honor, bring me through it, and I will continue to praise Him through it all."

PERSEVERANCE

> *Beloved, think it not strange concerning the fiery trial which is to try you, as though some strange thing happened unto you: but rejoice, inasmuch as ye are partakers of Christ's sufferings; that, when His glory shall be revealed, ye may be glad also with exceeding joy. If ye be reproached for the name of Christ, happy are ye; for the Spirit of glory and of God resteth upon you...* (1 Peter 4:12-14).

David asked the question, "Why?" He went on to say, "The kings of the earth set themselves against God's anointed." (See Psalms 2:1-2.) As we have learned, it is necessary for the anointed to suffer. When you begin to understand this principle of the Kingdom, it will cause you to rejoice in tribulation.

There is a root that produces an embalming agent the Bible calls *myrrh*. Myrrh was one of the major ingredients used by the priests and prophets to anoint and ordain people, places, and things that were set aside for the sacred service of the Lord. Myrrh is a fragrant substance. It grows from a small stick-like shrub. On the surface, there's nothing spectacular about it. It's not appealing to look upon. It is just a root-like shrub. Myrrh is also very bitter to taste. But if you throw it down on the ground and crush it, it exudes a lovely, wonderful, and heavenly fragrance.

The more you crush it, press on it, bruise it, and beat it, the more wonderful and delightful the scent that emanates. The more it becomes battered, bruised, and treaded upon, the more potent the release. It's nothing delightful to the eyes. It's a shattered root, but it sure smells good. God says in this hour to His servants, "If I'm going to use you to show forth My glory and My power, I'm going to have to crush you to extract My fragrance (the anointing) out of you. Trust Me in the crushing because when the crushing is all over with, it's going to bring about My purpose. I'm going to bring death so that I can bring life. I'm going to make you so aromatic that whenever you come into a room people will know that they have encountered someone who has been in the presence of

Almighty God."

God wants you filled and flowing with His anointing so much that He can send you into the stinky places of this world. When you enter these places, you will bring forth life that flows from the fragrance of God's presence.

POWER

People will know they encountered the presence of God.

LIVING

Lazarus is an example of this principle. He was dead. Lazarus' sisters said, "Lord, by now he stinketh!" Jesus took His time to see about His dying friend, Lazarus. The sisters thought Jesus' arrival was too late. They, like us, had not yet learned how to trust God in waiting. But when the aroma of Jesus' anointing hit the graveyard, the power of His anointing brought life where there was death. If Jesus had not specifically called Lazarus by name, everyone and everything would have risen. God's Word and Spirit force life into existence. God says, "I'm going to sweeten you up so when you go in the fragrance of My presence, you will fill the entire atmosphere. The place will light up because you walked in."

If you want to be anointed—if you want to receive the

power for living—you've got to be crushed. If you want to be anointed, you're going to have to go through some things. Have you been through something? If you really want to be blessed by the anointing, let somebody who has been through something preach, teach, or sing. If you are among all of those who say hallelujah just to be saying hallelujah because a man or woman of God preaches, you don't have any flavor. All of you who have been beaten, battered, shaken, crushed, rejected, and ostracized have a fragrance coming out of you sweeter than the honey in the honeycomb. It's better than the Rose of Sharon—unto God a sweet-smelling savor in His nostrils. And the more you're afflicted, the more anointed you will become.

Be Ye Steadfast

> *Therefore, my beloved brethren, be ye steadfast, unmoveable, always abounding in the work of the Lord, forasmuch as ye know that your labour is not in vain in the Lord* (1 Corinthians 15:58).

POWER POINTS FOR LIVING

1. You are more than a conqueror through Jesus Christ who loves you! What have you conquered lately? What do you plan to conquer in the near future? The far future?

2. You are the righteousness of God in Christ Jesus! Explain.

3. Greater is He who is in you than he who is in the world! Memorize this verse and stand on it during tough times.

4. You have the power to tread upon serpents and scorpions and over all the power of the enemy! You have the power—how will you release it?

5. No weapon formed against you shall prosper! (See Isaiah 54:17.) Satan's weapons are useless against the children

of God. Look up Ephesians 6:13-17 to read about your armor. Are you wearing yours today?

6. You really are the head and not the tail, above and not beneath, the rich and not the poor! How does this statement differ from what some in society think about Christians?

7. God will make you so aromatic that whenever you come into a room people will know that they have just encountered the presence of Almighty God. Do you reflect God's presence? Why or why not?

CHAPTER 11

GO FORTH WITH POWER!

And being let go, they went to their own company, and reported all that the chief priest and elders had said unto them. And when they heard that, they lifted up their voice to God with one accord, and said, Lord, Thou art God, which hast made heaven, and earth, and the sea, and all that in them is: who by the mouth of Thy servant David hast said, Why did the heathen rage, and the people imagine vain things? The kings of the earth stood up, and the rulers were gathered together against the Lord, and against His Christ. For of a truth against Thy holy child Jesus, whom Thou hast anointed, both Herod, and Pontius Pilate, with the Gentiles, and the people of Israel, were gathered together, for to do whatsoever Thy hand and Thy counsel determined before to be done. And now Lord, behold their threatenings: and grant unto Thy servants, that with all boldness they may speak Thy word, by stretching forth Thine hand to heal; and that signs and wonders may be done by the name of Thy holy child Jesus. And when they had prayed, the place was shaken where they were assembled together; and they were all filled with the Holy Ghost, and they spake the word of God with ***boldness*** (Acts 4:23-31, emphasis added).

Peter and John had been in jail for preaching the Gospel and healing a lame man in the name of Jesus. The Bible says that God had been greatly glorified in the hearts of the people as a result of the miracle the Lord had wrought through Peter and John. The rulers of the city sought to punish the apostles for preaching in Jesus' name, but God had come through and performed a miracle on their behalf, granting their release.

Now you know how it is when the Church comes under persecution. They come to fellowship services acting real funny! So Brother Peter said to himself, *I better get a good message for this service. Let me pull something here from the Book of Psalms. I'll use the passage when King David was all perplexed and confused, asking the Lord, "Why do the heathen rage?"*

Peter began to preach this message to them about God and purpose. Peter and John still had the prints of chains on their wrists, had been in jail all night long, and had probably been without food or water. Here was a chance to really be downtrodden and discouraged. Instead, Peter, the former "Teacher's pet," started preaching to them about purpose. He began (and I paraphrase): "You know folks, we just had a wonderful experience of God's Spirit as we were partying (celebrating) at the Pentecost festival, and as expected, we ran into a little trouble with the law for jamming (singing and praising) too loud, too hard, and too strong. We experienced a trial that caused us a little bit of pain and discomfort, but you're going to see God turn it around and make it work for your good."

POWER

If you pursue God's purpose, God's going to bless you with a divine destiny.

LIVING

The people were listening to Peter preach. Peter was excited, telling them about God's purpose. Peter continued, "Brethren, if you just pursue God's purpose, God's going to bless you with a divine destiny. God's going to show you how to come out of this. He is going to reveal to you how to be delivered." The Bible said that when they heard the Word, all of a sudden they began to believe what God had said about them. Let me say this, you've got to believe that you're coming out of your dilemma. You've got to believe that you're coming out of your trial and test with a passing and perfect score.

Do you know what happened when Peter got through preaching about God's purpose in their lives and answering their *whats* and *whys?* The Bible said that they got together and prayed. They prayed and prayed and prayed. They prayed until the whole house was shaken. They prayed until the floor began to shake. They prayed until the foundation began to tremble.

When you're praying for God's deliverance, you can't be praying little cute and sophisticated prayers. When you're in a desperate and urgent situation, an educational, intellectual, and dignified sounding prayer won't cut it.

POWER

They prayed until the floor began to shake.

LIVING

When you are really in trouble, you don't have time for those superficial, cute, impressive, and intellectual-sounding types of prayers like: "Oh, thou everlasting Father, Ruler of the universe, the I AM that I AM of Israel, the Consolation, the Hope of the world, the Mighty One. I come unto your auspicious grace, through the torn veil that was rent in the Temple. I lay my particulars before Your abilities, because through necessity I am able to determine Your preeminent preexistent greatness, and I lay before You the desires of my most fragile heart, knowing that Thou are always attentive to the prayers of Thy saints. Oh, Most Merciful...."

God says, "Shut up that insincere and phony mess!" When you are in real need of help, you don't have time for all that junk. What you need is a desperate "Help, Lord!

Please help now!" That other nonsense may be all right for some backward preacher trying to impress a bunch of flaky religious people, but when you are in serious trouble, burdened with a serious need, you've got to pray until you go beyond the limit of your flesh. You've got to pray until your will begins to line up with His will, until your thoughts become God's thoughts and your ways become His ways.

POWER

"I AM that I AM—
the Hope of the world."

LIVING

Sometimes we're confronted with problems and situations that are so complex that they very often go beyond our ability to understand and comprehend. That's exactly why the apostle Paul said, *"...the Spirit also helpeth our infirmities: for we know not what we should pray for as we ought: but the Spirit itself maketh intercession for us with groanings which cannot be uttered"* (Rom. 8:26). By infirmities, Paul means human weakness that indicates the inability to produce the desired results or fulfill the necessary need. The notation for infirmities in the *Ryrie Study Bible*, as it relates to Romans 8:26, says that these particular infirmities are "our inability to pray intelligently about 'certain' situations."

Regardless of how well you know the Word, and regardless of how prolific you are at praying and quoting the Word, you've got to know that there will come a time when you will not know what it is that you need in order to rectify a situation in accordance with the will of God. As the saints of God, if we are serious about submitting to and obeying the will of God for our lives, we need to have total reliance upon the Holy Spirit to direct us in all our daily affairs, "*... because He* [the Spirit] *maketh intercession for the saints according to the will of God"* (Rom. 8:27).

They prayed and the place they were assembled in began to shake. God filled them with the Holy Ghost and they started speaking the Word with boldness. The basic adherence to the "Word of Faith" doctrine, contrary to all the doomsayers, is a true and authentic biblical principle. However, you can't just speak the Word out of your flesh and expect it to work the will of God for your life. You have got to be, without exception, led of the Spirit in all that you do in God. The Bible says that "*... the letter killeth, but the Spirit giveth life"* (2 Cor. 3:6). That's what most of the New Testament is—letters. The Word and the Spirit must always be one together, not one without the other. The two must agree.

When the disciples prayed, they were filled with the Spirit of God. "Well," you might say, "I've already been baptized with the Spirit of God. I've already been filled. I even speak with new tongues!" That may be so, but are you filled with His Spirit and His power and glory now? I know you might have been baptized and filled with the Spirit years ago when you first got saved, but are you filled now? If not, He'll fill you again. To everyone and everybody who opens up to Him, God says, "I will fill them." To everybody who says, "I'm thirsty!" God says, "I'll fill them." Anyone whose cry is, "Lord, I'm longing for Your presence," God says, "I'll fill you." God wants to fill you until you get bold, until timid folks get bold, nervous folks get bold, and scared folks get bold. God says, "I'm gonna fill you until you go tell of the grace and goodness of the Lord."

POWER

God filled them with the Holy Ghost and they spoke the Word with boldness.

LIVING

Christ seemed to have no problem rebuking the enemy who came against Him. It was after the victory was won that He needed the ministry of angels to continue His vision. There are some people who have not been released from old trials yet because they will not allow God to heal them through the angels of ministry He has chosen to use.

Some have been through so much that they simply don't trust anymore. They need *someone*, but they don't trust *anyone*.

> *And He was there in the wilderness forty days, tempted of Satan; and was with the wild beasts; and the angels ministered unto Him* (Mark 1:13).

What impresses me the most is that in order for Christ to receive the ministry of angels, He had to allow the lesser (the angels) to minister to the greater (the Christ). He allowed the angels whom He created, the same angels He commanded as Captain of the host, to minister to Him. My friend, when pain peaks, you don't care who God uses! You just want to be healed and blessed. If you were in an automobile accident and you needed help, you wouldn't care who the paramedics were. Their education, denomination, or ethnic background would mean nothing to you because of the enormity of your need.

Whenever we seek His will, we must be prepared to receive His way!

Speak the Word

You need to speak the Word of God with boldness, not with your feelings, your problems, or situations. You need to set your mind on God's promise and God's Word, and begin to speak the Word of God with boldness. We need not let external circumstances and situations dictate our feelings, behavior, and mindset. Stop believing what others say and start believing what the Word of God says. What does the Word say?

If you are always weeping over rejection and misunderstanding; if you're always upset over who doesn't accept you into their circles anymore, you may be suffering from an immunity deficiency syndrome. You waste precious time of communion when you ask God to change the minds of people. It is not the people or the pressure that must change, it is you. In order to survive the stresses of success, you must build up an immunity to those things that won't change.

Thank God that He provides elasticity for us. Remember, you can't switch price tags just because you don't like the price. My constant prayer is, "Lord, change me until this doesn't hurt anymore." I am like David—I am forever praying my way into the secret place. The secret place in the king's court was called a pavilion. There you are insulated from the enemy. If you could make it to the secret place, all hell could break loose outside, but it would not matter to you, for in the secret place there is peace. If you want to accomplish much, if you intend to survive Cain's hateful children, then you need to get in the secret place and stay there!

> *For in the time of trouble He shall hide me in His pavilion: in the secret of His tabernacle shall He hide me; He shall set me up upon a rock* (Psalms 27:5).

God's Word declares, "My God shall supply all my needs according to His riches in glory by Christ Jesus... The Lord is my shepherd and I shall not want...By His stripes I am healed...If any man be in Christ he is a new creature, old things have passed away, all things have become new...The earth is the Lord's and the fullness thereof, and they that dwell therein." Speak the Word; speak the Word! If the Word said you shall have whatever you say, then you shall have whatever you say. I dare you to say it.

> *The Lord is my light and my salvation: whom shall I fear? The Lord is the strength of my life; of whom shall I be afraid? When the wicked, even mine enemies and my foes, came upon me to eat up my flesh, they stumbled and fell. Though an host should encamp against me, my heart shall not fear: though war should rise against me, in this will I be confident. One thing have I desired of the Lord, that will I seek after; that I may dwell in the house of the Lord all the days of my life, to behold the beauty of the Lord and to inquire in His temple. For in the time of trouble He shall hide me in his pavilion: in the secret place of His tabernacle shall He hide me; He shall set me up upon a rock. And now shall mine head be lifted up above mine enemies round about me: therefore will I offer in His tabernacle sacrifices of joy; I will sing, yea, I will sing praises unto the Lord. Hear, O Lord, when I cry with my voice: have mercy also upon me, and answer me. When Thou saidst, Seek ye My face; my heart said unto Thee, Thy face, Lord, will I seek* (Psalms 27:1-8).

Obviously, if you've read this book up to this point, you have issues in your life that you've been seeking answers about—you've been seeking the power for living that God has promised. I pray that what has been said in these pages will be used by the Spirit of God to give you understanding and peace about the present course of your life. If you don't have peace, I pray that because of what you've read, you will feel free to petition and request of the Lord answers for your situation.

POWER

If you don't have peace, feel free to petition and request of the Lord answers for your situation.

LIVING

God has given us all purpose and reason for our own individual lives. We are truly a people of destiny. You need to pursue your destiny by the will and grace of God. But understand and know assuredly that your destiny has a price. It's not without cost. What is the cost? It costs you everything. I close with the words of a late, great, wise man:

If you want a thing bad enough to go out and fight for it, to work day and night for it, to give up your time, your peace, and sleep for it. If all that you dream and scheme is about it. If life seems useless and worthless without it. If you'd gladly sweat for it, fret for it, and plan for it. If you lose all your terror of the opposition for it. If you're willing to simply go after the thing you want with all your capacity and tenacity, faith, hope and confidence, and stern personality. If neither cold, famine, poverty, sickness, nor pain of body or mind can keep you from the thing you want. If dogged and determined you besiege and beset it, with the help of God, you will get it!

Go forth with the power for living life to the fullest!

POWER POINTS FOR LIVING

1. You've got to believe that you're coming out of your trial and test with a passing and perfect score. Do you?

2. You need to speak the Word of God with boldness, not with your feelings, your problems, or situations. Do you have a habit of explaining your problems rather than shouting your blessings?

3. Stop believing what others say and start believing what the Word of God says. Father God knows you and loves you better than *anyone*. What steps can you take to listen more closely to what He has to say about you?

4. As the saints of God, if we are serious about submitting to and obeying the will of God for our lives, we need to have total reliance upon the Holy Spirit to

direct us in all our daily affairs. What part does the Holy Spirit play in your life?

5. You have got to be, without exception, led of the Spirit in all that you do in God. Are you willing to make this commitment?

6. God will supply all your needs according to His riches in glory by Christ Jesus. Do you believe this? What are you trusting Him for today?

7. Pursue your destiny by the will and grace of God—who gives you the power to live victoriously!

PART II

POWER PRINCIPLES

These powerful principles are offered as small but mighty doses of energy to propel you through 30 days of triumphant living. These devotionals equip your mind and spirit to accept any and all challenges that may come your way.

Because each begins with an inspiring Scripture passage, these quick-starts to your day (morning, afternoon, or evening) can be referred to time and time again for wisdom and comfort.

PRINCIPLE 1

For a just man falleth seven times, and riseth up again: but the wicked shall fall into mischief (Proverbs 24:16).

Sometimes Christians become frustrated and withdraw from activity on the basis of personal struggles. They think it's all over, but God says, "Not so!" The best is yet to come. But if you want the Lord to come, you mustn't tell Him that you aren't planning to get up.

The whole theme of Christianity is one of rising again. However, you can't rise until you fall. Now that doesn't mean you should fall into sin. It means you should allow the resurrecting power of the Holy Ghost to operate in your life regardless of whether you have fallen into sin, discouragement, apathy, or fear. But it doesn't matter what tripped you; it matters that you rise up. People who never experience these things generally are people who don't do anything. There is a certain safety in being dormant. Nothing is won, but nothing is lost. I would rather walk on the water with Jesus. I would rather nearly drown and have to be saved than play it safe and never experience the miraculous.

PRINCIPLE 2

Not only so, but we also rejoice in our sufferings, because we know that suffering produces perseverance; perseverance, character; and character, hope (Romans 5:3-4 NIV).

Relentless is a word I use to describe people who will not take no for an answer! They try things one way, and if that doesn't work, they try it another way. But they don't give up. You who are about to break beneath the stress of intense struggles—be relentless! Do not quit!

A terrible thing happens to people who give up too easily. It is called regret. It is the nagging, gnawing feeling that says, "If I had tried harder, I could have succeeded." Granted, we all experience some degree of failure. That is how we learn and grow. The problem isn't failure; it is when we fail and question whether it was our lack of commitment that allowed us to forfeit an opportunity to turn the test into a triumph! We can never be sure of the answer unless we rally our talents, muster our courage, and focus our strength to achieve a goal. If we don't have the passion to be relentless, then we should leave it alone.

PRINCIPLE 3

But we have this treasure in earthen vessels, that the excellency of the power may be of God, and not of us (2 Corinthians 4:7).

Many Christians struggle to produce a premature change when God-ordained change can only be accomplished according to His time. We cannot expect to change the flesh. It will not respond to therapy. God intends for us to grow spiritually while we live in our vile, corrupt flesh. While we are changed in our spirit by the new birth, our old corruptible body and fleshly desires are not. It is His will that our treasure be displayed in a cabinet of putrid, unregenerated flesh—openly displaying the strange dichotomy between the temporal and the eternal.

It is amazing that God would put so much in so little. The true wonder of His glory is painted on the dark canvas of our old personhood. What a glorious backdrop our weakness makes for His strength!

There is a great deal of *power* released through the friction of the holy graces of God grating against the dry, gritty surface of human incapacities and limitations. We sharpen our testimonies whenever we press His glory against our struggles.

PRINCIPLE 4

Even so ye, forasmuch as ye are zealous of spiritual gifts, seek that ye may excel to the edifying of the church (1 Corinthians 14:12).

You would be surprised to know how many people there are who never focus on a goal. They do several things haphazardly without examining how forceful they can be when they totally commit themselves to a cause. The difference between the masterful and the mediocre is often a focused effort. On the other hand, mediocrity is masterful to persons of limited resources and abilities. So in reality, true success is relative to ability. What is a miraculous occurrence for one person can be nothing of consequence to another. A person's goal must be set on the basis of his ability to cultivate talents and his or her agility in provoking a change.

I am convinced that I have not fully developed my giftings. I am committed to being all that I was intended and predestined to be for the Lord, for my family, and for myself. How about you—have you decided to roll up your sleeves and go to work?

Remember, effort is the bridge between mediocrity and masterful accomplishment!

PRINCIPLE 5

Stand fast therefore in the liberty wherewith Christ hath made us free, and be not entangled again with the yoke of bondage (Galatians 5:1).

When Christ taught in the temple courts, there were those who tried to trap Him in His words. They knew that His ministry appealed to the masses of lowly people. They thought that if they could get Him to say some condemning things, the people wouldn't follow Him anymore.

The blood of Jesus is efficacious, cleansing the woman who feels unclean. How can we reject what He has cleansed and made whole? Just as He said to the woman then, He proclaims today, *"Neither do I condemn thee: go and sin no more."* How can the Church do any less?

The chains that bind are often from events that we have no control over. Other times the chains are there because we have willfully lived lives that bring bondage and pain.

Regardless of the source, Jesus comes to set us free. He is unleashing His Church. He forgives, heals, and restores. All can find the potential of their future because of His wonderful power operating in their lives.

PRINCIPLE 6

O Lord, how many are my foes! . . . But You are a shield around me, O Lord; You bestow glory on me and lift up my head. To the Lord I cry aloud, and He answers me from His holy hill. Selah (Psalms 3:1, 3-4 NIV).

David declares that it is the Lord who sustains you in the perilous times of inner struggle and warfare. It is the precious peace of God that eases your tension when you are trying to make decisions in the face of criticism and cynicism. When you realize that some people do not want you to be successful, the pressure mounts drastically. Many have said, "God will not deliver him." However, the mere fact that many are saying it doesn't make it true.

I believe that the safest place in the whole world is in the will of God. If you align your plan with His purpose, success is imminent! On the other hand, if I have not been as successful as I would like to be, then seeking the purpose of God inevitably enriches my resources and makes the impossible attainable.

If the storm comes and I know I am in the will of God, then little else matters.

PRINCIPLE 7

Against Thee, Thee only, have I sinned, and done this evil in Thy sight: that Thou mightest be justified when Thou speakest, and be clear when Thou judgest (Psalms 51:4).

Saul was anointed by God to be king. He was more moral than David in that he didn't struggle in some of the areas that plagued David. His weakness wasn't outward; it was inward. Saul looked like a king, whereas David looked like an underage juvenile delinquent who should have been home taking care of the flocks. Saul's armor shined in the noonday sun. David had no armor. Even his weapon looked substandard; it was just an old, ragged, shepherd's slingshot.

Although David's weapon was outwardly substandard, it was nevertheless lethal; it led to the destruction of the giant. We can never destroy our enemy with the superficial armor of a pious king. We don't need the superficial. We need the supernatural! David's naked, unassuming demeanor was so transparent that he often seems to us extremely vulnerable. You would almost think he was unfit, except that when he repents, there is something so *powerful* in his prayer that even his most adamant critic must admire his openness with God!

PRINCIPLE 8

And the scribes and Pharisees brought unto Him a woman taken in adultery; and when they had set her in the midst, they say unto Him, Master, this woman was taken in adultery, in the very act.... So when they continued asking Him, He lifted up Himself, and said unto them, He that is without sin among you, let him first cast a stone at her (John 8:3-4,7).

Clearly Jesus saw the foolish religious pride in their hearts. He was not condoning the sin of adultery. He simply understood the need to meet people where they were and minister to their need. He saw the pride in the Pharisees and ministered correction to that pride. He saw the wounded woman and ministered forgiveness. Justice demanded that she be stoned to death. Mercy threw the case out of court. Jesus knew *the power of a second chance.*

There are those today who are very much like this woman. They have come into the Church. They have been stoned and ridiculed. They may not be physically broken and bowed over, but they are wounded within. Somehow the Church must find room to throw off condemnation and give life and healing.

PRINCIPLE 9

As one whom his mother comforteth, so will I comfort you; and ye shall be comforted in Jerusalem (Isaiah 66:13).

I remember when our car broke down. It didn't have too far to break down because it was already at death's door. At the time, though, I needed to get uptown to ask the electric company not to cut off the only utility I had left. I pleaded with them but they cut it off anyway. I was crushed. I had been laid off my job, and my church was so poor it couldn't even pay attention. I walked out of the utility office and burst into tears. I looked like an insane person walking down the street. I was at the end of my rope.

To this melodramatic outburst God said

absolutely nothing. He waited until I had gained some slight level of composure and then He spoke. He said, "I will not suffer thy foot to be moved!" I shall never forget as long as I live the peace of His promise that came into my spirit. Suddenly the light, the gas, and the money didn't matter. What mattered was that I knew I was not alone.

PRINCIPLE 10

And He arose, and rebuked the wind, and said unto the sea, Peace, be still. And the wind ceased, and there was a great calm (Mark 4:39).

Have you allowed God to stand in the bow of your ship and speak peace to the thing that once terrified you? We can only benefit from resolved issues. The great tragedy is that most of us keep our pain active. Our power is never activated because our past remains unresolved. If we want to see God's power come from the pain of an experience, we must allow the process of healing to take us beyond bitterness into a resolution that releases us from the prison and sets us free.

To never trust again is to live on the pinnacle of

a tower. You always talk about the past because you stopped living years ago. Listen to your speech. You discuss the past as if it were the present because the past has stolen the present right out of your hand! In the name of Jesus, get it back!

God's healing process and power make us free to taste life again, free to trust again, and free to live without threatening fears.

PRINCIPLE 11

In whom also we have obtained an inheritance, being predestinated according to the purpose of Him who worketh all things after the counsel of His own will (Ephesians 1:11).

Have you reached that place in life where you enjoy your own company? Have you taken the time to enjoy your own personhood? When other people give affirmation, it reflects their opinion about you. When they leave, you may feel worthless and insignificant. But when you speak comfort and blessings to yourself, it reflects your own opinion about yourself. The best scenario is to enjoy both kinds of affirmation.

There are reasons to give yourself a standing

ovation. The first is the fact that your steps are carefully observed and arranged by God Himself. They are designed to achieve a special purpose in your life. The Bible says, *"If God be for us, who can be against us?"* (Rom. 8:31b). So you must rejoice because you are in step with the beat of Heaven and the purposes of God. Second, you ought to rejoice because you are pursuing a goal that defies human manipulation. Your blessing rests in accomplishing the will of God through His powerful anointing.

PRINCIPLE 12

Let your light so shine before men, that they may see your good works, and glorify your Father which is in heaven (Matthew 5:16).

It is wonderful to have a plan, but that means nothing if you have no power to perform the plan and accomplish the purpose. God sends people in and out of your life to exercise your faith and develop your character. When they are gone, they leave you with the reality that your God is with you to deliver you wherever you go! Moses died and left Joshua in charge, but God told him, "*...As I was with Moses, so I will be with thee...*" (Josh. 1:5). Joshua never would have learned that while Moses was there. You learn this kind of thing when "Moses" is gone. *Power is developed in the absence of human* *assistance.* Then we can test the limits of our resourcefulness and the magnitude of the favor of God.

There is within the most timid person—beneath that soft, flaccid demeanor—a God-given strength that supersedes any weakness he appears to have. The Bible puts it this way: *"I can do* ***everything*** *through Him who gives me strength!"* (Phil. 4:13 NIV, emphasis added).

PRINCIPLE 13

Not that I speak in respect of want: for I have learned, in whatsoever state I am, therewith to be content (Philippians 4:11).

If you are praying, "Lord, make me bigger," you are probably miserable, although prayerful. Did you know you can be prayerful and still be miserable? Anytime you use prayer to change God, who is perfect, instead of using prayer to change yourself, you are miserable. Instead, try praying this: "Lord, make me better." I admit that better is harder to measure and not as noticeable to the eye. But better will overcome bigger every time.

What a joy it is to be at peace with who you are and where you are in your life. I want to be better—to have a better character, better confidence, and a better attitude! The desire to be bigger will not allow you to rest, relax, or enjoy your blessing. The desire to be better, however, will afford you a barefoot stroll down a deserted beach. Thank God for the things that you know He brought you through.

Thank God for small things.

PRINCIPLE 14

For you know that we dealt with each of you as a father deals with his own children, encouraging, comforting and urging you to live lives worthy of God, who calls you into His kingdom and glory (1 Thessalonians 2:11-12 NIV).

Isn't it amazing how we can see so much potential in others, yet find it difficult to unlock our own hidden treasure? Nurturing is the investment necessary to stimulate the potential that we possess. Without nurturing, inner strengths may remain dormant. Therefore it is crucial to our development that there be some degree of nurturing the intrinsic resources we possess.

There is a difference in the emotional makeup of

a child who has had a substantial deposit of affection and affirmation. Great affirmation occurs when someone invests into our personhood. Anyone will invest in a sure success, but aren't we grateful when someone supports us when we are somewhat of a risk?

Unfortunately, nothing brings luster to your character and commitment to your heart like opposition does. The finished product is a result of the fiery process. It creates someone who shines with the kind of brilliancy that enables God to look down and see Himself.

PRINCIPLE 15

But He knoweth the way that I take: when He hath tried me, I shall come forth as gold (Job 23:10).

We spend most of our time talking about what we want from God. The real issue is what He wants from us. It is the Lord who has the greatest investment. We are the parched, dry ground from which Christ springs. Believe me, God is serious about His investment!

God will fight to protect the investment He has placed in your life. What a comfort it is to know that the Lord has a vested interest in my deliverance. God has begun the necessary process of cultivating what He has invested in my life. Have you ever stopped to think that it was God's divine purpose that kept you afloat when others capsized beneath the load of life? Look at Job; he knew that God had an investment in his life that no season of distress could eradicate.

Have you ever gone through a dilemma that should have scorched every area of your life, and yet you survived the pressure? Then you ought to know that He is Lord over the fire!

PRINCIPLE 16

When thou passest through the waters, I will be with thee; and through the rivers, they shall not overflow thee: when thou walkest through the fire, thou shalt not be burned; neither shall the flame kindle upon thee (Isaiah 43:2).

It has been suggested that if you walk in the Spirit, you won't have to contend with the fire. Real faith doesn't mean you won't go through the fire. The presence of the Lord can turn a burning inferno into a walk in the park! The Bible says a fourth person was in the fire, and the three Hebrews were able to walk around unharmed in it (see Dan. 3).

King Nebuchadnezzar was astonished when he

saw them overcome what had destroyed other men. I cannot guarantee that you will not face terrifying situations if you believe God. I can declare that if you face them with Christ's presence, the effects of the circumstance will be drastically altered. If you believe God, you can walk in what other men burn in. Seldom will anyone fully appreciate the fire you have walked through, but God knows the fiery path to accomplishment. He can heal the blistered feet of the traveler.

PRINCIPLE 17

For he hath regarded the low estate of His handmaiden: for, behold, from henceforth all generations shall call me blessed (Luke 1:48).

I believe it is important that women get healed and released in their spirits. I believe God will move freshly in the lives of women in an even greater way.

God knows how to take a mess and turn it into a miracle. If you're in a mess, don't be too upset about it, because God specializes in fixing messes. God is saying some definite things about women being set free and delivered to fulfill their purpose in the Kingdom.

When the Lord gets through working on you, all

your adversaries will be ashamed. The people who contributed to your sense of low self-esteem will be ashamed when God gets through unleashing you. You won't have to prove anything. God will prove it. He will do it in your life. When He gets through showing that you've done the right thing and come to the right place, they will drop their heads and be ashamed.

If you have a past that torments you, Jesus can set you free. He *will* unleash your potential.

PRINCIPLE 18

The Lord is my light and my salvation; whom shall I fear? The Lord is the strength of my life; of whom shall I be afraid? When the wicked, even mine enemies and my foes, came upon me to eat up my flesh, they stumbled and fell (Psalms 27:1-2).

Sometimes pain can become too familiar. Ungodly relationships often become familiar. Change doesn't come easily. Habits and patterns are hard to break. Sometimes we maintain relationships because we fear change. However, when we see our value the way Jesus sees us, we muster the courage to break away.

He will defend you before your critics. Now is the time for you to focus on receiving the miraculous and getting the water that you could not get before. He is loosing you to water. You haven't been drinking for years, but now you can get a drink. With Jesus, you can do it.

Some of you have been a pack horse for many years. People have dumped on you. You've never been allowed to develop without stress and weights, not just because of the circumstances, but because of how deeply things affect you.

Our God, however, is a liberator.

PRINCIPLE 19

The eyes of your understanding being enlightened; that ye may know what is the hope of His calling, and what the riches of the glory of His inheritance in the saints (Ephesians 1:18).

You want the inheritance of your earthly father to pass on to you. So, why should you sit there and be in need when your heavenly Father has left you everything? Your Father is rich, and He left everything to you. However, you will not get your inheritance until you ask for it. Demand what your Father left you. That degree, that promotion, that financial breakthrough has your name on it.

The power to get wealth is in your tongue. You shall have whatever you say. If you keep sitting around murmuring, groaning, and complaining, you use your tongue against yourself. Open your mouth and speak something good about yourself. Speak deliverance and *power*. You are not defeated.

When you start speaking correctly, God will give you what you say. Say what you want. God willed you something. Your Father left you an inheritance.

PRINCIPLE 20

For His anger endureth but a moment; in His favour is life: weeping may endure for a night, but joy cometh in the morning (Psalms 30:5).

David said that if we could hold out, joy comes in the morning. The bad news is, everybody has a bad night at one time or another. The good news is there will be a morning after. Allow the joy of the morning light to push away any unwanted patterns, curses, or fears that stop you from achieving your goal.

So let the hungry mouth of failure's offspring meet the dry breast of a Christian who has determined to overcome the past. In order for these embryos of destruction to survive, they must be fed.

They feed on the fears and insecurities of people who haven't declared their liberty.

Once you realize that you are the source from which it draws its milk, you regain control. Feed what you want to live and starve what you want to die! Why not think positively until every negative thing that is a result of dead issues turns blue and releases its grip on your home and your destiny? It's your mind.

You've got the *power*.

PRINCIPLE 21

...If there be any virtue, and if there be any praise, think on these things (Philippians 4:8).

In this verse to the Philippians, Paul teaches thought modification. He taught that if we exercise the discipline of thought modification, we can produce internal or intrinsic excellence. The phrase, *"if there be any virtue,"* suggests that if there is to be any intrinsic excellence, we must modify our thoughts to think on the things he mentioned first.

The term *virtue* refers to intrinsic excellence. That means people who are filled with excellence achieve that excellence by the thoughts they have about themselves and about the world around them.

Thoughts are powerful. They feed the seeds of

greatness that are in the womb of our minds. They also can nurse the negative insecurities that limit us and exempt us from greatness, *"for as he thinketh in his heart, so is he …"* (Prov. 23:7).

There is a virtue that comes from tranquil, peaceful thoughts that build positive character in the heart. As a rule, people who are cynical and vicious tend to be unsuccessful. If they are successful, they don't really feel their success because their cynicism robs from them the sweet taste of reward.

PRINCIPLE 22

For the weapons of our warfare are not carnal but mighty in God for pulling down strongholds, casting down arguments and every high thing that exalts itself against the knowledge of God, bringing every thought into captivity to the obedience of Christ (2 Corinthians 10:4-5 NKJV).

God has given you power over the enemy! He has given you the power to abort the seeds of failure. Pull down those things that have taken a strong hold in your life. If you don't pull them down, they will refuse to relinquish their grip. It will take an act of *your will and God's power* to stop the spiritual unborn from manifesting in your life. God will not do it without you—but He will do it through you.

The greatest freedom you have is the freedom to change your mind. Repentance is when the mind decides to overthrow the government that controlled it in the past. As long as these other things reign in your life, they are sitting on the throne. If they are on the throne, then Christ is on the Cross. Put Christ on the throne and your past on the Cross.

PRINCIPLE 23

Before I formed thee in the belly I knew thee; and before thou camest forth out of the womb I sanctified thee, and I ordained thee a prophet unto the nations (Jeremiah 1:5).

Salvation as it relates to destiny is the God-given power to become what God has eternally decreed you were before the foundation of the world. Grace is God's divine enablement to accomplish predestined purpose. When the Lord told Paul, *"My grace is sufficient for thee..."* (2 Cor. 12:9), His power was not intimidated by Paul's circumstances.

You are empowered by God to accomplish goals that transcend human limitations! It is important that each person God uses realizes that they are able to accomplish what others cannot only because God gives them the grace to do so. Problems are not really problems to a person who has the grace to serve in a particular area.

The excellency of our gifts is of God and not of us. He doesn't need nearly as much of our contribution as we think He does. So it is God who works out our internal destinies. He gives us the power to become who we are eternally and internally.

PRINCIPLE 24

But now, O Lord, Thou art our father; we are the clay, and Thou our potter; and we all are the work of Thy hand (Isaiah 64:8).

Where is the God who sent an earthquake into the valley of dry bones and put them together? (See Ezekiel 37.) Or where is the God of the clay, who remolds the broken places and mends the jagged edge? (See Isaiah 64:8.) The God we seek is never far away. The issue is not so much His presence as it is my perception. Many times deliverance doesn't cost God one action. Deliverance comes when my mind accepts His timing and purpose in my life.

In my hours of crisis, many times I found myself searching for the place of rest rather than for the answer. If I can find God, my needs become insignificant in the light of His presence. What is a problem if God is there? Do you realize the *power* of God's presence? I hear many people speak about the acts of God, but have you ever considered the mere *presence* of God?

He doesn't have to do anything but be there, and it is over!

PRINCIPLE 25

I thank my God always on your behalf, for the grace of God which is given you by Jesus Christ (1 Corinthians 1:4).

And when Jesus saw her, He called her to Him, and said unto her, Woman, thou art loosed from thine infirmity. And He laid His hands on her: and immediately she was made straight, and glorified God.... And when He had said these things, all His adversaries were ashamed: and all the people rejoiced for all the glorious things that were done by Him (Luke 13:12-13,17).

Praise is contagious. Those who saw Jesus heal the infirm woman were caught up in praise as well. The Church also must join in praise when the broken are healed. Those who missed the great blessing that day were those who decided to argue about religion.

Christ unleashed *power* in the infirm woman that day. He healed her body and gave her the strength of character to keep a proper attitude. The woman who is broken today will find power unleashed within her too, when she responds to the call and brings her wounds to the Great Physician.

PRINCIPLE 26

Behold, happy is the man whom God correcteth: therefore despise not thou the chastening of the Almighty: for He maketh sore, and bindeth up: He woundeth, and His hands make whole. He shall deliver thee in six troubles: yea, in seven there shall no evil touch thee (Job 5:17-19).

Listen for God's hammering in the spirit. It appears that He is not there, but He is.

Perhaps you've said, "Where is the move of God that I used to experience? Why am I going through these fiery trials?" God is there with you even now. He is operating in a different realm.

I know so well how hard it is to trust Him when you can't trace Him! But that's exactly what He wants you to do—He wants you to trust Him. It may seem that everybody is passing you right now. Avoid measuring yourself against other people. God knows when the time is right. His methods may seem crude and His teachings laborious, but His results will be simply breathtaking. Without scams and games, without trickery or politics, God will accomplish a supernatural miracle because you trusted Him while He worked in the invisible realm.

PRINCIPLE 27

Above all else, guard your heart, for it is the wellspring of life (Proverbs 4:23 NIV).

Be aware that the enemy is trying to steal something from you that is not visible. Any time the invisible is stolen, its absence is not readily detected. On what day does passion leave a marriage? On which morning did the worker lose interest in his job? At what point does the customer decide, "I am not going to buy this product"?

The only solution lies in the absolute, committed guarding of the heart. Your greatest treasure isn't your certificate of deposit. It isn't your retirement, or your stocks and bonds. Your greatest treasure is in the strength of the passion that is locked in the recesses of your heart. Out of the heart flow the issues of life.

You must keep a firm sobriety about you, warming your heart with it like it was a warm coat on a wintry night. Keep a sobriety that refuses to become drunken with fear, discontentment, or insecurity. Wrap your godly attitude closely around your heart, for it is the wellspring or the resource from which comes the power to keep on living and giving!

PRINCIPLE 28

He brought me to the banqueting house, and his banner over me was love (Song of Solomon 2:4).

I hope you can relate to what a blessing it is to be alive, to be able to feel, to be able to taste life. Lift the glass to your mouth and drink deeply of life; it is a privilege to experience every drop of a human relationship. It is not perfect; but the imperfection adds to its uniqueness. I am sure yours, like mine, is a mixing of good days, sad days, and all the challenges of life.

I hope you have learned that a truly good relationship is filled with dreams and pains and tender moments. Moments that make you smile secret smiles in the middle of the day. Moments so strong that they never die, yet are so fragile they disappear like bubbles in a glass. It does not matter whether you have something to be envied or something to be developed; if you can look back and catch a few moments, you are blessed! You could have been anywhere doing anything but instead the maitre d' has seated you at a *table for two*!

PRINCIPLE 29

And wisdom and knowledge shall be the stability of thy times, and strength of salvation: the fear of the Lord is His treasure (Isaiah 33:6).

There ought to be a threefold celebration going on in your heart right now. First, you ought to look back over your times of obscurity, when He was plowing and fertilizing you, and thank God that you are still here to attest to His sustaining power. A lesser vessel would not have survived your testimony.

Second, look around you at the blessings that you have right now. With a twinkle in your eye and a melody in your heart, thank God for what He is doing even at this moment. Your freshly cultivated ground is full of seeds and unborn potential.

Third, you should celebrate what God is about to do in your life. Your heart ought to be thumping in your chest; your blood ought to be racing like a car engine about to peel rubber! You are about to step into the greatest harvest of your life. You were created for this moment—and this moment was created for you!

Do you know what time it is?

It's your time!

PRINCIPLE 30

Now he that ministereth seed to the sower both minister bread for your food, and multiply your seed sown, and increase the fruits of your righteousness (2 Corinthians 9:10b).

I pray that this word is so powerful and personal, so intimate and applicable, that it leaves behind it a barren mind made pregnant. This seed of greatness will explode in your life and harvest in your children, feeding the generations to come and changing the winds of destiny.

As we move on to other issues and face our inner selves, we strip away our facades and see ourselves as we really are. We need to not be fearful of our nakedness nor discouraged by our flaws.

In my heart I smell an approaching rain. Moisture is in the air and the clouds have gathered. Our fields have been chosen for the next rain and the wind has started to blow. Run into the field with your precious seeds and plant them in the soft ground of your fertile mind. Whatever you plant in the evening will be reaped in the morning.

I am so excited for you. I just heard a powerful clap of thunder...in just another moment, there'll be rain!

Bonus Material

RELEASE YOUR ANOINTING

CHAPTER 1

POWER FOR LIVING

Why is it so important to pray with the power of the Holy Ghost? All too often the spirit is willing, but our flesh is weak. We need God's help to overcome the tug of our carnal nature.

The spirit is willing but our flesh is weak.

Being filled with the Holy Ghost places the power of God at our disposal to carry out the work of the Kingdom. Soon after being baptized in the Holy Ghost, most believers notice a marked change in their ability to pray and walk in God's anointing.

HUMANKIND IS BODY, SOUL, AND SPIRIT

Apostle Paul wrote:

> *And I pray God your whole spirit and soul and body be preserved blameless unto the coming of our Lord Jesus Christ* (1 Thessalonians 5:23).

This Scripture shows us the three parts of humankind: body, soul, and spirit.

If these three parts were the same, Paul never would have prayed that each of them would be wholly preserved. If we want to have a successful prayer life and reach our full potential with God, then each of these parts must be understood and put in their place.

Each of these parts affects our prayer life. If we were only spirit, the blessings of prayer would be unrestrained, without hindrance. But we also have to deal with the body and soul.

The words *wholly* and *preserved* are significant. *Wholly* means to completely, absolutely reach the limit or potential. *Preserved* means to guard, to watch, to keep an eye on, to keep something in its place. As we pray, we must contend with these three parts. Each element plays a significant role in the success or failure of our prayer life:

1. Body

The body entails our flesh and its appetites. The flesh never wants to pray. The flesh never awakens you with a desire to seek God. The flesh is at enmity with God and does not understand His ways. This is why no one can please God in the flesh. Because the flesh will never come up to the expectations of the spirit, we must discipline the flesh to be subject to what we know is right. The flesh will sit back and say, "You don't have to pray. If it's going to happen, then it will happen." But we must go into combat to get certain things. We must bombard the gates of Heaven to obtain certain things, and the body never wants to do this.

2. Soul

The soul of man is sandwiched between the body, which never wants to pray or do right, and the spirit, which desires God and spiritual things. The soul entails our emotions, feelings, weaknesses, and our past. An ongoing, progressive, renewing work occurs in your soul. When we pray with our soul, we pray with our intellect and an understanding to the best of our ability. But to go into deep spiritual warfare, we must go beyond our logic and our intellect.

3. Spirit

When you were lost, your spirit was *"dead in trespasses and sins"* (Eph. 2:1). Now that you are saved, however, your spirit has been quickened, which means "to vitalize, to cause to live, to be vibrant and strong." As the Holy Ghost begins to have an intimate relationship with our spirit, we begin to produce the *"fruit of the Spirit"* (see Gal. 5:22-23). The Holy Ghost wants to know you in an intimate way; He doesn't want just a surface relationship.

> *Adam knew his wife again; and she bare a son, and called his name Seth* (Genesis 4:25).

Intimacy results in fruit, or offspring.

Apostle Paul wrote, *"that I may know him…"* (Phil. 3:10), which implies a close relationship, one that causes us to partake in His experiences. But you can't know Christ in resurrection power until you know Him in His sufferings and death. Our old man must be crucified with Him daily as we are being changed from glory to glory.

Apostle Paul knew Jesus in the pardon and forgiveness of sin, but still longed to know Him intimately. For this to occur, two things had to happen.

- *"Forgetting those things which are behind"* (Phil. 3:13). These were not all bad or questionable activities, but they were not satisfying either. They left Paul crying out for more of God.
- *"Reaching forth unto those things which are before"* (Phil. 3:13). Paul wanted to *"…press toward the mark for the prize of the high calling of God in Christ Jesus"* (Phil. 3:14). He wanted to become spiritually intimate with Jesus to produce fruit.

Why Speak in Tongues?

This is a good question asked by many intelligent people. Why should anyone speak in tongues? Tongues merely express the language of God. In order for us to reach the will of God for our lives, we must be able to communicate with God.

We must communicate with God.

Speaking in tongues is not a strange new doctrine. In fact, it's been around for hundreds, even thousands, of years. God poured it out at the inception of the Church.

Before we cover several scriptural reasons for this practice, I would like to share an example that highlights the importance of speaking in tongues.

A CB radio gives you the ability to speak to other people providing you are on the same frequency. Different people use different channels for a variety of reasons. Whatever channel you use to transmit or receive a message, the transmitter and the one receiving the message must be on the same channel and have the squelch turned up loud enough to hear. CB radios also have a special channel for emergencies. Any time you need the police or emergency assistance you can switch to this frequency and no one else can monitor your conversation.

This may seem like a crude analogy, but in the spirit world many messages are being transmitted. The Bible says that satan is the *"prince of the power of the air"* (Eph. 2:2). If we stay on the same frequency, he can pick up our transmissions. But satan cannot monitor the emergency channel. His squelch cannot tune in because it is just a bunch of static to him. He cannot make out what we are saying. Praying in the Spirit is a frequency that satan cannot pick up.

Bypassing Satan's Radar

> *And I heard a loud voice saying in heaven, Now is come salvation, and strength, and the kingdom of our God, and the power of his Christ: for the accuser of our brethren is cast down, which accused them before our God day and night* (Revelation 12:10).

Since satan is the prince of the power of the air and comes before the presence of God, he constantly surveys our prayer life. No wonder we experience such adversity and opposition when we try to get close to God. To make our way to the throne of God, we must push past the enemy's surveillance.

> *For we wrestle not against flesh and blood, but against principalities, against powers, against the rulers of the darkness of this world, against spiritual wickedness in high places* (Ephesians 6:12).

Let me use another illustration. In the first Iraq War, the United States and their allies knew that they were up against some of the most modern, up-to-date defenses in all the world.

The war was waged in two parts. During the first part, known as Desert Watch or Desert Shield, the United States flew reconnaissance flights to monitor the movement and the strengths and weaknesses of the enemy.

Because of these reconnaissance flights, we learned that Iraq had employed the most modern, state-of-the-art radar systems. The United States knew that if we were to be successful—with limited casualties—we would have to somehow bypass Iraq's radar system. This was achieved by using stealth bombers, which enabled us to mount an attack without being detected on radar.

On the first night of the attack, the major bombardment was almost over before Iraq even realized what had happened.

When you pray in the Spirit, you go before the throne of God undetected by satan because you speak mysteries to Him. Your prayers are like stealth bombers that bypass satan's detection.

Your prayers are like stealth bombers bypassing satan.

Praying in the Spirit enables you to pray healing, delivering, yoke-breaking, devil-stomping prayers without being shot at. You can go into God's presence and receive ammunition to shake the gates of hell. That's why satan fights people from praying in the Spirit. He confuses people regarding this truth because he knows he doesn't have a weapon to defend against it.

SWITCH CHANNELS

> *The apostle Paul uses the word* ***tongues*** (plural) *to show his multiplicity of languages. "Though I speak with the tongues of men and of angels..."* (1 Corinthians 13:1).

Sometimes we need to speak in our natural language according to our heritage. Sometimes, however, our natural language is no match for the warring spirits between earth and the throne of God.

When prayers in our natural language are being intercepted and shot down, Paul tells us to switch channels. Allow the Holy Ghost within you to speak out on earth what Heaven is speaking into your spirit. This is praying in tongues, or praying in the Spirit.

Satan understands the language of men. When we pray about a certain thing, our adversary causes principalities and powers in the atmosphere between earth and the throne of God to intercept our words. He attacks the very thing we pray about.

Satan does not understand the language of Heaven. God's ways, which are so much higher than our ways, include praying in tongues. This leaves satan confused as to how to attack us. He may assign an evil spirit to attack our prayer life and report back to him so he can make a counterattack. But when we pray in the Spirit, or pray in tongues, we frustrate his plans.

Remember that tongues are spiritual and not fleshly. Satan works through our flesh. When our prayers switch from an earthly, fleshly, carnal language to a secondary, spiritual, heavenly language, satan is confused.

The believer is built up as the Holy Ghost pleads the life, the power, the joy, and the victory of God into your spirit. Hallelujah for the ability to speak out from earth what the Holy Ghost is speaking in from Heaven!

Interceding With Groans

Speaking in tongues places a great arsenal of spiritual weaponry at your disposal. Not knowing this, however, causes many believers to struggle in prayer and intercession.

> *Likewise the Spirit also helpeth our infirmities: for we know not what we should pray for as we ought: but the Spirit itself maketh intercession for us with groanings which cannot be uttered. And He that searcheth the hearts knoweth what is the mind of the Spirit, because He maketh intercession for the saints according to the will of God* (Romans 8:26-27).

Romans 8:26 contains a word that is often overlooked, and that is the very first word, *likewise*. The word means "in like manner, or to be similar to."

> *For we know that the whole creation groaneth and travaileth in pain together until now. And not only they, but ourselves also, which have the firstfruits of the Spirit, even we ourselves groan within ourselves, waiting for the adoption, to wit, the redemption of our body* (Romans 8:22-23).

The word *likewise* points back to the two previous times the word *groan* is used in that chapter. Romans 8:22 refers to the groan of creation waiting for the redemption and restoration of this earth. Romans 8:23 refers to the groans of Christians as we await the completion of our redemption, the receiving of our new body.

Apostle Paul uses the same word for the groans of the Holy Ghost (vs. 26). The word *groanings* means "to groan with a sigh, or a sense of lamenting."

This was very familiar to the Old Testament prophets. When they got in tune with the nature and character of God, they often expressed themselves in unusual ways. Their intercession for the people could be described as wailing, howling, or lamenting. They were speaking a language outwardly that God was speaking inwardly to them.

We cannot understand the language of God in our own intellect.

I like to explain it like this: When a child who cannot talk plainly wants something, he or she may be able to speak only portions of words. A stranger may not understand, but the child's mother can make out the language. Even though the baby talk is barely intelligible, she understands the need. Taking a bunch of stammering, broken remarks, she interprets the language to meet the need.

We cannot understand the language of God in our own intellect.

Sometimes in order to get what you need from God, you must go from one language (our human intellect) to another language (the Holy Ghost).

HELP IN PRAYER

The Holy Ghost stands alongside us to assist, to cause one to stand, to cause one to achieve. As the *Helper*, He stands in covenant with us. In essence, the Holy Ghost stands by your side to not only plead the covenant of God, but to cause you to attain what the covenant provides for you.

He does this in four ways:

1. He assists us through our infirmities. The Spirit *"helpeth our infirmities"* (Rom. 8:26), which means He stands alongside as an ally, one waiting in the wings who is willing and able to assist us. We need help because *"the spirit indeed is willing, but the flesh is weak"* (Matt. 26:41).

   The word *infirmities* means "inability to produce results." Opposition prevents you from receiving what God has provided for you in His covenant. The Holy Ghost helps us and gives us a break-through.
2. He assists us in that He knows; the Holy Spirit is very knowledgeable about things that perplex us. *"For we know not what we should pray for"* (Rom. 8:26). We don't always know what is right. As we allow the Holy Ghost to saturate and to permeate our lives, He begins to tell us how to pray for certain things.

   For instance, whom should you date? Whom should you marry? Where should you go to church? In what ministry should you serve? Sometimes you'll want to speak or do something and the Holy Ghost will caution you, "Don't say or do that." He assists you when you don't have clear direction.

3. He assists us with intercessions. As Jesus our Mediator pleads us to God, the Holy Ghost, who knows the very mind of God, pleads God to us. He *"maketh intercession for us"* (Rom. 8:26). *Intercession* means that the Holy Ghost will meet with us. He comes into our situation and speaks into our spirit as one who interviews another.

   We don't have the ability to produce results and to get our breakthrough. Even if we did have the ability, we are still void of knowledge because we "know not what we should pray for." The Holy Ghost will get us to admit our frailties. Then He will fellowship with us and assist us in what to do. As the Holy Ghost intercedes, He merely speaks into earth what He has already heard spoken in the counsels of Heaven.

   This is why Jesus often repeated a truth He wanted to reveal—"Verily, verily" or "Truly, truly"—once in the heavenlies by divine sanction, and once in the earth to carry out the divine sanction.

4. He assists us with Heaven's language. The Spirit pleads the will of God to us. *"He maketh intercession for the saints according to the will of God"* (Rom. 8:27). As creation groans, it speaks a language that only God can interpret. The saints of God sometimes groan with broken, stammering remarks.

Sometimes all we can do is lay before God, not knowing what to do or say. We need to be full of the Holy Ghost and listening to Him because He will plead God's will to us. We just have to be able to hear. *"He that hath an ear, let him hear what the Spirit saith unto the churches"* (Rev. 2:7).

The Holy Ghost pleads God's will to us.

The Holy Ghost Relays What Heaven Sends

John 16:13 presents some of the greatest truths ever revealed to the Church:

> *Howbeit when He, the Spirit of truth, is come, He will guide you into all truth: for He shall not speak of Himself; but whatsoever He shall hear, that shall He speak: and He will shew you things to come.*

Jesus said the Holy Ghost would do four things:

1. He will guide you into all truth.
2. He will speak truth to you, but He will not speak of Himself.
3. He will show you all truth concerning things to come.
4. He will speak into you what He hears Heaven speaking into Him.

We must be able to hear what the Holy Ghost is saying to be able to release our anointing. But it is equally important to know the Holy Ghost hears what to speak to us. He never breaks the chain of command from Heaven. How can we know that what the Holy Ghost says is reliable?

First, the Holy Ghost is one with God. He will never speak anything that is not sanctioned by the Word. Second, God, who cannot lie, searched Heaven and earth for someone to confirm His covenant and swear to its authenticity. When He could find no one else to meet the criteria of His holy demands, God swore by Himself. Now the Holy Ghost freely speaks a sworn oath and covenant into the hearts of Spirit-filled believers who can hear His voice.

Jesus said, *"whatsoever He shall hear, that shall He speak."* That means the Holy Ghost speaks into you what Heaven has already decreed.

Build Up Yourself

In the following passage we find some of the simplest and most profound truths in all the Word of God. But everything hinges on the truth stated in verse 20:

> *But ye, beloved, building up yourselves on your most holy faith, praying in the Holy Ghost, keep yourselves in the love of God, looking for the mercy of our Lord Jesus Christ unto eternal life. And of some have compassion, making a difference: and others save with fear, pulling them out of the fire; hating even the garment spotted by the flesh* (Jude 20-23).

We can build up ourselves, cultivate a sense of expectancy about the coming of the Lord, have compassion on those who have fallen, and be moved with zeal to make a difference in the lives of those who have spotted their garments.

Let's look at the ability to "build up." The word *build* is an architectural word that means "to cause a building to stand." It means "to lay a good foundation." In the natural realm, it is always important to leave yourself the ability to add on to your building in case you need to expand in the future. If you have outgrown your spiritual house, the Holy Ghost gives you the resources to add on to meet your demands.

If you have more ministry, then you have a place to house it, to build on. Are there weak areas in the structure? Build them up. You do this by praying in the Holy Spirit. This will build up your faith so that you can stand against Goliath and know that your God is bigger than the giant who defies you.

When God got ready to bless Elijah, His ultimate will was for the prophet to stand on Mt. Carmel; *Carmel* means "fruitful ground." But the blessing came progressively as he went to the brook Cherith where he drank from its waters and was fed by ravens. One day, however, the brook dried up and no longer met his needs. The word *cherith* means "to make covenant with." God made a covenant, proving not only Himself to Elijah, but Elijah to Himself.

Next, God sent Elijah to a widow in Zarephath. *Zarephath* means "to refine as in a melting pot." Gold is not pure in its original form and must be refined, which is done by heating it to boiling. The heat separates the raw substance from its impurities, which surface to the top and are skimmed off. God does the same for us, using the heat of trials to separate the gold from the dross in our lives.

Call down fire from Heaven!

God leads you through a progressive path, but the ultimate goal is to be on Mt. Carmel and be fruitful. He wants you to be able to call fire down from Heaven, to see into the Spirit as Elijah saw, and to persevere in prayer until God intervenes in your situation. The answer to your drought may appear to be a cloud the size of a man's hand, but you know a refreshing rain is about to fall.

This is why Christians from all denominations are being filled with the Holy Ghost. Having outgrown the tradition of their past experiences, they have passed the tests at Cherith and Zarephath and are ready to go to Mt. Carmel.

If you feel a hunger to go on with God, the Holy Ghost is telling you that your present spiritual house is too small. He is urging you to build upon your present foundation. In order to do this, however, we must pray in the Holy Ghost.

More Benefits

Unlike giving a message in tongues in a public meeting, which edifies other people, praying in tongues edifies you. Praying in tongues does at least five things for you as an individual:

1. Praying in tongues gives you the ability to talk to God alone, frustrating the devil. *"He that speaketh in an unknown tongue speaketh not unto men, but unto God"* (1 Cor. 14:2). This gives you the ability to bypass all others and go into the presence of God. The Old Testament equivalent would be to go into the

holy of holies and commune directly with God.

Your adversary brings certain things against you to discourage and cause you to lose focus. Praying in tongues enables you to bypass his radar system.

2. Praying in tongues edifies the person praying (see 1 Cor. 14:4). The word *edify* means "to build up, to build on, to establish a structure." As you pray in tongues, you enlarge your borders. If you have more ministry than prayer life, then add on. If you have outgrown where you are, then add on.

Add on!

Your complexes will vanish as the Holy Ghost imparts confidence. Your fears will vanish as the Holy Ghost builds you up. Your past failures and sins will be dealt a decisive blow by the Holy Ghost. This change will take every weak area in your structure and begin to brace and strengthen it, giving you glorious victory.

You may not even notice the change taking place, and you might not even realize it's the Holy Ghost doing the work quietly and internally. But it won't be long before what is happening on the inside begins to manifest itself on the outside. As you learn to pray in the Holy Ghost, it will just happen automatically.

As you come into a deeper relationship with God, you will find that you cannot survive on a "Now I lay me down to sleep" prayer. Your prayer life will have to match your ministry and commitment to Spirit-filled living.

> *But ye, beloved, building up yourselves on your most holy faith, praying in the Holy Ghost* (Jude 20).

Praying in the Holy Ghost shores up the foundation of our faith.

The best defense against disease is our natural immune system, which has been designed by God to help us ward off the enemies of our body and diseases that come against us. But the immune system must be kept strong and vibrant by eating right, getting plenty of rest, and exercising.

Many of us are at our lowest point spiritually and have become susceptible to anything that comes our way. But if we pray in the Holy Ghost, we will be built up, enabling us to fight off sin and discouragement.

> *And take the helmet of salvation, and the sword of the Spirit, which is the word of God: praying always with all prayer and supplication in the Spirit, and watching thereunto with all perseverance and supplication for all saints* (Ephesians 6:17-18).

3. Praying in tongues helps you put on the armor of God. Many Christians feel this spiritual preparation is like choosing their clothes for the day from their closet. The apostle Paul mentioned our warfare, our enemies, and our armor, which covers every vital part of a soldier: the helmet (our mind); the breastplate (our heart); the girdle of truth (the truth of God's Word upon which the whole armor rests); the shield of faith, which kept the soldier walking

forward and never turning his back, which was exposed; the preparation of the Gospel on our feet (our walk). This armor dresses us for any occasion.

The full description of the armor and its relationship to prayer is given in Ephesians 6:13-18, but the key is found in verses 17 and 18. After describing the armor piece by piece, Paul goes right from verse 17 to verse 18 without stopping. It's as if he's saying, "This is how you get the armor: praying always in the Spirit." Praying in the Holy Ghost clothes us from head to foot with the armor of God. Yes, praying in the Spirit arms you with an arsenal that will cause you to stand. Hallelujah for the ability to pray in the Holy Ghost!

4. Praying in tongues builds up a wall of defense.

> *When the enemy shall come in like a flood, the Spirit of the Lord shall lift up a standard against him* (Isaiah 59:19).

Yes, there are times when the enemy invades our lives. He will come into your mind; he will come into your marriage; he will come into your ministry. He comes in like a flood and desires to devour you and anything that has been born of God in your life.

The Holy Spirit stands by as your ally. When the enemy comes in like a flood, the Spirit shall lift up a standard against him. He provides you with a place of defense, a place of shelter, a place of refuge, a place to hide.

The Holy Spirit is your strongest ally.

Job's life is a good example of this. When God praised Job's integrity, satan pointed out:

> *Hast not thou made an hedge about him, and about his house, and about all that he hath on every side?...* (Job 1:10).

The adversary asked permission to touch all that Job had. Satan came in like a flood, destroying Job's sons, daughters, servants, and livestock. Not satisfied with this, satan asked permission to afflict Job's body. God set a limit, however, and said, "*...Save his life*" (Job 2:6).

Praying in the Spirit sets up a wall of defense that satan cannot penetrate. The Spirit will lift up the wall of the blood of Jesus and say, "Satan, you can't touch this!"

5. Praying in tongues helps you relieve anxiety.

> *Come ye yourselves apart into a desert place, and rest a while* (Mark 6:31).

Praying in the Spirit allows you to come apart before you come apart. Many of you are under severe pressure. You are tense, battle-weary. Like the disciples, you need a solitary place to rest awhile.

Spirit praying separates us from worldly pressures.

Praying in the Spirit pulls us into an experience with God and enables us to release our anointing. It's not surprising that Paul wondered whether he was in the body or out of the body. The apostle saw and heard things unlawful for a man to speak. God in the Spirit takes us to paradise, pulling us apart from the pressures of the world before we come apart.

A piece of material does not come apart suddenly. It unravels bit by bit. If you don't repair it, a small tear can cause the whole garment to come apart. Praying in the Spirit brings us to that solitary place with God to help cope with stress, pressure, and anxiety. If your life is falling apart, your need is similar to the woman with the issue of blood. She wanted to touch the hem of Christ's garment. She realized the hem was where all loose ends were put back together. This is what praying in the Spirit will do.

Praying in the Spirit brings peace.

What is it then? I will pray with the spirit, and I will pray with the understanding also: I will sing with the spirit, and I will sing with the understanding also (1 Corinthians 14:15).

"I will pray with the spirit" means that your spirit is engaged as you rely on the Holy Ghost to guide you in prayer. He will speak, but we must listen. When we pray according to the leading of the Holy Spirit, we are praying with the knowledge of God's will:

> *Likewise the Spirit also helpeth our infirmities: for we know not what we should pray for as we ought: but the Spirit itself maketh intercession for us with groanings which cannot be uttered* (Romans 8:26).

We also pray with the insight of the Spirit:

> *And he that searcheth the hearts knoweth what is the mind of the Spirit, because he maketh intercession for the saints according to the will of God* (Romans 8:27).

When we pray in the Spirit, we pray with fervency and intensity as the Spirit gives us the unction. He helps us to focus on what we are praying for and diligently seek God.

> *But without faith it is impossible to please him: for he that cometh to God must believe that he is, and that he is a rewarder of them that diligently seek him* (Hebrews 11:6).

"I will pray with the understanding" means that as we

pray by the unction and leadership of the Holy Ghost, we pray a prayer that will have meaning as the same Holy Ghost interprets to us the things that we have spoken.

Sometimes we have no knowledge of how to pray because the things that we confront are bigger than we are. They are deeper than our human logic can comprehend.

That's why we need to pray within the spirit realm, which is bigger than any problem, weakness, or dilemma we face. We also need to ask God to interpret to us the things that we have spoken through the auspices of the Holy Ghost. As He reveals them to us, we will gain an understanding.

We Need the Anointing

Sometimes we don't know what to say. When your heart is crushed and your spirit is overwhelmed, you know that you need a touch. You know the area that needs to be touched, but you don't always know what to say.

Have you ever been so overwhelmed, so overcome that all you can do is groan? Maybe you can only say, "Jesus, help me," or "I need You, Lord." That's when we need to change our language. We need to wait on the Holy Ghost because He knows how to pray—and what to pray. The Holy Ghost will always pray in alignment with the will of God (see Rom. 8:27).

The anointing of the Holy Ghost doesn't always bring chills or goose bumps. It isn't always charged with emotion. The anointing, however, brings power.

The Old Testament high priest knew there was only one place where he could see and experience a manifestation of God's glory and that was in the holy of holies. That's where God promised to show Himself and commune with His people (see Exod. 25:17-22).

In these last days, satan and all his cohorts are waging a final onslaught against the Church. We must know God in a way in which we have never known Him before. Within some of you are miracles, unborn babies, ministries, and gifts. We all have callings.

The anointing brings power.

Because of circumstances—perhaps something beyond your control; perhaps because of your faults, failures, or your past life—satan has told you that your baby, your gift, your ministry, must be aborted. But satan is a liar. Scripture tells us *"the gifts and callings of God are without repentance"* (Rom. 11:29). You need to get to where you can see the raw, undiluted presence of God and His anointing. Only then can you release your anointing to bring glory to His Kingdom.

You Can Make It!

What encourages me when I go through the storms of life? I look in the Word of God and find that someone else has already been there and made it through. We are surrounded by witnesses:

> *Wherefore seeing we also are compassed about with so great a cloud of witnesses, let us lay aside every weight, and the sin which doth so easily beset us, and let us run with patience the race that is set before us* (Hebrews 12:1).

In each instance, however, these saints had to get to a certain place before they saw the manifestation of God.

Noah endured a torrential downpour that flooded the earth for months, but he had a place that gave him access to God. On the third level of the ark a window gave him access to the heavenlies.

> *A window shalt thou make to the ark, and in a cubit shalt thou finish it above; and the door of the ark shalt thou set in the side thereof; with lower, second, and third stories shalt thou make it* (Genesis 6:16).

In the midst of his storm Noah found solace and peace.

Jacob struggled for years with who he was, compared with who he wanted to be. His wrestling climaxed when he got to Jabbok, which means "to pour out, to empty." Jacob went alone to Jabbok, the place of struggle where he wrestled with an angel. Divinity met with humanity, and Jacob's thigh was put out of joint. Upon arriving at the place, the patriarch was known as Jacob (swindler, supplanter, cheater), but after the struggle, his name was Israel (prince of God). It was a place of power, as God gave him power with Himself and man. (See Genesis 32:21-29.)

Moses struggled with his leadership responsibilities over the nation of Israel. The demands of the multitude taxed Moses to the point of exhaustion. Moses asked God for a manifestation of His glory. But before Moses could see this manifestation, he had to get to a certain place. Hidden in the cleft of a rock, Moses saw the afterglow of God's glory, but only after he got to that place.

How the Anointing Works

If you're a believer in Christ, you have some type of calling on your life. You may be a pastor or a leader in the church. You may have a specific gift that needs to be stirred up.

You have a calling.

Like Jacob, you may be struggling with who you are. Some of you may be wrestling with your past. You need to know that there is a place with God of yoke-breaking anointing. Let's look at two passages of Scripture for some timely truths:

Behold, how good and how pleasant it is for brethren to dwell together in unity! It is like the precious ointment upon the head, that ran down upon the beard, even Aaron's beard: that went down to the skirts of his garments; as the dew of Hermon, and as the dew that descended upon the mountains of Zion: for there the Lord commanded the blessing, even life for evermore (Psalms 133:1-3).

And it shall come to pass in that day, that his burden shall be taken away from off thy shoulder, and his yoke from off thy neck, and the yoke shall be destroyed because of the anointing (Isaiah 10:27).

1. The anointing flows from the head down (see Ps. 133:2). Jesus is the head. His anointing is flowing, but we must be in alignment (in fellowship) with Him.
2. The anointing will be *"as the dew of Hermon"* (Ps. 133:3a). The Israelites knew the dew of Mt. Hermon and Mt. Zion was heavy even in dry weather.
3. The anointing will take authority over your situations. *"For there the Lord commanded the blessing"* (Ps. 133:3b).

4. The anointing will lift burdens from your shoulder (see Isa. 10:27a).
5. The anointing will take away yokes that have caused you to say and do things and go places you really didn't desire (see Isa. 10:27).
6. The anointing will destroy the yoke. It isn't enough to just lift the yoke from your neck. If you leave a yoke enabled, it can resume its previous position at any time. The anointing dismantles everything that satan had planned for your life (see Isa. 10:27).

In the days of the judges, the Philistines stole the Ark of the Covenant. They placed the Ark beside their god, Dagon. The presence of God in the Ark caused Dagon to fall on his face. After the Philistines sat him up again, the presence of God caused Dagon to fall a second time. Upon his second fall his head and the palms of both his hands were cut off. (See First Samuel 5:1-4.)

Everything satan planned to do (his head) and all the things he wanted to do (his hands) has been destroyed by the anointing. He has been cut off and rendered helpless.

> *No weapon that is formed against thee shall prosper; and every tongue that shall rise*

> *against thee in judgment thou shalt condemn. This is the heritage of the servants of the Lord, and their righteousness is of me, saith the Lord* (Isaiah 54:17).

This level of anointing is vital because we will need to have high-level talks with God that we do not want satan to hear or to understand. We need the ability to change languages. Tongues are available, and they are for you. You can speak the language as the Spirit of God gives the utterance.

THE MASTER KEY

As long as we operate according to human logic and our carnal perceptions of things, we will find ourselves up and down with our circumstances. But when we tap into the Holy Ghost, our knowledge takes on a whole new perspective and we begin to operate in Kingdom authority.

Tap into the Holy Ghost for wisdom.

We no longer fret when the gates of hell rise up against us because we know that Jesus has given us the master key, which is the anointing of the Holy Ghost. You don't have to worry about being locked in or locked out if you have the master key. The master key can open any lock.

Jesus told Peter not to worry about the gates of hell because He would give him the keys to the Kingdom (see Matt. 16:17-19). These keys were a mystery to others, but to Peter the keys solved any dilemma because they were Kingdom keys. They were a mystery to some, but a message of prevailing authority to those who understand the code.

Jesus faced these four dilemmas:

1. The traditions of men (see Matt. 15:1-3).
2. Outward religion that left the heart desperately wicked (see Matt. 15:10-20).
3. Physical infirmities, a type (or symbol) of spiritual handicaps (see Matt. 15:29-31).
4. Physical hunger, a type (or symbol) of spiritual starvation and famine (see Matt. 15:32-39).

Jesus asked His disciples, *"Whom do men say that I the Son of man am?"* (Matt. 16:13). Understanding the answer to this question opened the way to an anointing that left the gates of hell powerless.

They answered:

> *Some say that Thou art John the Baptist: some, Elias; and others, Jeremias, or one of the prophets* (Matthew 16:14).

These were merely fleshly men with limitations.

Then Jesus asked, *"But whom say ye that I am?"* (Matt. 16:15). Peter confessed, *"Thou art the Christ, the Son of the living God"* (Matt. 16:16). The Greek word for *Christ* is *Christós,* the anointed one from God.

The anointing renders satan powerless.

Jesus knew these four types of crises had left the people in hopeless situations. They were trying to handle these four areas by seeing Jesus as just an earthly man, a teacher, or a prophet. These four dilemmas had left them victims locked in a prison without a key.

When we recognize Jesus as the Christ, however, He gives us a master key (the anointing) to unlock any crisis in our life. The anointing does not promise to keep the gates of hell from coming against you, but it prevents the gates of hell from prevailing against you.

Everything Has a Price

When you shop, you know that everything has a price tag. As you peruse the merchandise in stores, you probably ask yourself some very basic questions:

1. Do I need this particular item?
2. Can I afford the price?

3. Does it have a warranty?
4. Would I use it if I bought it?

The value of the anointing can be understood with these same four guidelines.

1. We desperately need the anointing of the Holy Ghost.
2. The Holy Ghost is well worth the price.
3. The Holy Ghost has a warranty sealed unto the day of redemption.
4. In order to fulfill everything that a sovereign God has ordained for our lives, we must use the power of the Holy Ghost to reach our potential and destiny.

Jesus Christ knew the importance of being anointed for works of service. He quoted the prophet Isaiah at the outset of His ministry:

> *The Spirit of the Lord God is upon Me; because the Lord hath anointed Me to preach good tidings unto the meek; He hath sent Me to bind up the brokenhearted, to proclaim liberty to the captives, and the opening of the prison to them that are bound; to proclaim the acceptable year of the Lord, and the day*

> *of vengeance of our God; to comfort all that mourn; to appoint unto them that mourn in Zion, to give unto them beauty for ashes, the oil of joy for mourning, the garment of praise for the spirit of heaviness; that they might be called trees of righteousness, the planting of the Lord, that He might be glorified* (Isaiah 61:1-3).

May we cry out for an infilling of the Holy Ghost that we might be enabled to pray in the Spirit and walk in a greater anointing. Like our Master, may we be anointed *"with the Holy Ghost and with power"* (Acts 10:38).

Cry out for a Holy Ghost infilling!

Esther 1:1; 2-12

Amos 5:15.
Proverbs 3:5-6
Jeremiah 8:9